The Twilight Zone
The Complete Episode Guide

Nick Naughton

CONTENTS

4 - Preface

5 - The Time Element

8 - Season One
51 - Season Two
87 - Season Three
135 - Season Four
161 - Season Five

205 - Final Lists

208 - References

PREFACE

The Twilight Zone was created by the great Rod Serling and ran from 1959 for 156 episodes. At its very best it was the gold standard by which other fantasy anthology shows are still judged. The following book offers a guide to every episode of The Twilight Zone - including a synopsis, trivia, and an evaluation and ranking. Hopefully this book will provide a valuable reference guide to all the episodes for anyone interested in this wonderful show. At the conclusion of this book I will offer a few lists of the best and the worst of the episodes.

My rankings and opinions are of course subjective. You may enjoy some of these episodes more (or indeed less!) than I did but the book that follows will hopefully help to separate the wheat from the chaff and give you an indication which stories should be at the top (and bottom) of the pile for any prospective Twilight Zone marathon. So, without further delay, let's take a deep dive into the mysterious, spine-tingling, fantastical, occasionally whimsical, and wonderful world of The Twilight Zone...

THE TIME ELEMENT (Director: Allen Reisner, Writer: Rod Serling) 1958

"Once upon a time there was a psychiatrist named Arnold Gillespie and a patient whose name was Peter Jenson. Mr. Jenson walked into the office nine minutes ago. It is eleven o'clock, Saturday morning, October 4th, 1958. It is perhaps chronologically trite to be so specific about an hour and a date but involved in this story is a time element."

The Time Element is what you might describe as the unofficial Twilight Zone pilot. This story was sold to CBS by Rod Serling and adapted for television as part of the Westinghouse Desilu Playhouse. CBS were initially said to be rather unenthusiastic about the script (it could be that the story revolving around Pearl Harbour, which was still fairly recent history at the time, might explain some of their wariness) and didn't exactly trip over themselves to adapt it but this changed when Bert Granet became a producer at CBS and desired an original Rod Serling script to adapt for television.

The Time Element, despite the apparent misgivings of CBS, happily generated a positive reception from viewers and led directly to The Twilight Zone. This is very much a blueprint for The Twilight Zone in that it has an outlandish premise and a haunting and memorable twist ending. The Time Element was broadcast on November 24, 1958, and was hosted and introduced by Desi Arnaz (who unnecessarily suggests a theory for the twist at the conclusion of the story). There are no opening and closing monologues by Rod Serling in The Time Element. The enjoyable tradition of the Serling monologues to frame the episodes would become a fundamental part of The Twilight Zone though. Despite feeling rather forgotten today, the Time Element is essentially like a bonus episode of The Twilight Zone for fans and very much a blood relative to the show that followed.

The premise of The Time Element concerns a man named Peter Jenson (William Bendix). Jenson, who seems exceptionally frazzled and agitated, visits psychoanalyst Dr Gillespie (Martin Balsam) to seek guidance on how to cope with the vivid and discombobulating dreams he has to endure night after night. More than anything Jenson simply wants to know if Dr Gillespie can provide any explanation for what is happening to him. In his dreams, Jenson find himself transported from the present day New York of 1958 to Honolulu in 1941. The specific date in 1941 is December the 6th - one day before the Japanese attack on Pearl Harbour.

Jenson tries to warn the people he meets in 1941 - most saliently a young newly married naval ensign named Janoski (Darryl Hickman) - that an attack is imminent but naturally no one believes him. Jenson's claim that he is from 1958 predictably make people think he is completely crazy. Jenson tells a dubious Dr Gillespie that these are not mere dreams. He is convinced that when he sleeps he REALLY is transported back to 1941...

The Time Element is a fairly absorbing fantastical drama that always manages to hold one's attention with its time travel premise. The Twilight Zone would return to the theme of time travel more than once (with mixed results) but The Time Element is a solid enough first riff on this well worn fantasy story device. The twist at the end of The Time Element is terrific and brings the story to a satisfying and hauntingly atmospheric conclusion. The Time Element is not perfect though. The most obvious problem is that it is an hour long - as opposed to the classic half-hour format (the fourth season aside) of The Twilight Zone.

One can't help feeling that The Time Element would have worked even better if edited down slightly. Though the scenes of Jenson and Dr Gillespie together are enjoyable it feels like there are a few too many of them. One might argue there are also a few too many scenes of a drunken Jenson becoming belligerent in the Honolulu bar he frequents. There is a very affecting scene though where Jenson - now desperate and at the end of his rope - breaks down in the bar and begins singing World War 2 songs that he assures the bewildered patrons they'll soon be all too familiar with.

William Bendix is a trifle overwrought at times as Jenson and the actors playing the young naval couple are not the most natural in the world but Martin Balsam (who would of course appear in The Twilight Zone more than once) is very good and the other supporting parts are generally well cast. The Time Element's direction is a little on the flat side. The Twilight Zone itself was more stylish and inventive than The Time Element in terms of its production. These quibbles aside though, The Time Element is very compelling at its best and definitely worth watching. As far as time travel stories go, The Time Element is not bad at all and the twist alone makes this worthy of your time. You can't help thinking that a half-hour version of The Time Element with Jack Klugman as Jenson might well have been a classic Twilight Zone episode. B

Season One 1959/1960

WHERE IS EVERYBODY? (Director: Robert Stevens, Writer: Rod Serling)

"The place is here, the time is now, and the journey into the shadows that we're about to watch could be our journey."

An amnesia stricken and confused man named Mike Ferris (Earl Holliman) wanders through a lonely, deserted landscape and seemingly abandoned town in an Air Force uniform with no memory of what may or may not have happened to present this mysterious state of affairs. As Mike becomes more and more spooked by his lonely and puzzling situation he begins to feel like someone is secretly watching him...

Rod Serling got the idea for Where Is Everybody? after wandering through an empty studio lot and finding it rather creepy. All the evidence of a community but no people anywhere - just a sense of desolation and loneliness. It struck him how unsettling and nightmarish it would be to suddenly find yourself alone in a city with no people whatsoever. It's very apparent that much care and effort has gone into this pilot. It cost $75,000 (a lot of money for a 30 minute television pilot in 1959) and was shot at Universal Studios over nine days. When the pilot was first screened to the network and sponsors it was deemed so strong that a deal was cut within six hours for The Twilight Zone to become a series.

Where Is Everybody? is a strong and intriguing start for what would soon become an iconic and justifiably famous series. The mystery device is perhaps not the most original but the premise works well and develops a surreal and strange atmosphere - especially in the scene where Ferris encounters an empty diner with recent evidence of activity and people having been there. Holliman's performance is effective enough to convince us of his desperate plight and this Twilight Zone's opener is well produced and committed to the premise it presents the viewer. This is a successful and interesting beginning for The Twilight Zone. Where Is Everybody? is certainly worthy of your time.

You may well guess the twist before it arrives but it still serves as a fairly effective way to wrap up the story. One notable thing about Where Is Everybody? is that the (soon to be familiar) opening narration was originally by Westbrook Van Voorhis rather than Rod Serling. They decided on reflection that Van Voorhis sounded rather too one note and pompous and approached Orson Welles to replace him. After Welles asked for a preposterous amount of money for his famous vocal services a very reluctant Rod Serling decided to do The Twilight Zone narrations himself. A happy accident. He was perfect and his voice became an integral and iconic part of the series. B+

ONE FOR THE ANGELS (Director: Robert Parrish, Writer: Rod Serling)

"Street scene: summer. The present. Man on a sidewalk named Lew Bookman, age sixtyish. Occupation: pitchman. Lew Bookman, a fixture of the summer, a rather minor component to a hot July, a nondescript, commonplace little man whose life is a treadmill built out of sidewalks. In just a moment, Lew Bookman will have to concern himself with survival, because as of three o'clock this hot July afternoon he'll be stalked by Mr Death."

Amiable low-rent salesman Lew Bookman (Ed Wynn) is visited by Death (Murray Hamilton) and told that his time is up. Lew (with slight shades of Bergman's then recent The Seventh Seal) manages to delay the inevitable by proposing that first he must first make his final masterpiece pitch as a salesman. The "one for the angels". When Lew fails to complete the pitch (for rather obvious reasons), Death reveals that he will take a young girl named Maggie (Dana Dillway) in his place. Lew must use all of his street smarts and cunning to outhink Death and save Maggie...

This was based on a teleplay Rod Serling wrote out of college about a sidewalk salesman who must save his brother from being whacked by some hoods by delivering such a brilliant series of sales pitches that he and his brother are always surrounded by crowds and so therefore safe. He juggled the plot details around, gave it an injection of fantasy and fashioned it as a Twilight Zone story and vehicle for the comedian Ed Wynn.

Wynn is far too deliberate and laid back to ever be terribly convincing as a salesman with fast persuasive patter but he delivers a likeable and sweet performance at the heart of the story. Wynn's warm hearted performance manages to wring a lot of charm from what is a relatively straight forward screenplay. What Serling does most successfully is make a grand noble hero out of what appears on the surface to be a most ordinary figure though - of course - Lew is no ordinary man. Children love Lew and in Serling's eyes this makes him a "very important" man. One For the Angels is not the most memorable Twilight Zone of this or any other era and fades in the memory fairly soon compared to the classic episodes but it's watchable enough with Wynn's loveable character negating the slightly over familiar premise. Far from a classic but a likeable little episode. B-

MR DENTON ON DOOMSDAY
(Director: Allen Reisner, Writer: Rod Serling)

"Portrait of a town drunk named Al Denton. This is a man who's begun his dying early - a long, agonizing route through a maze of bottles. Al Denton, who would probably give an arm or a leg or a part of his soul to have another chance, to be able to rise up and shake the dirt from his body and the bad dreams that infest his consciousness. In the parlance of the times, this is a peddler, a rather fanciful-looking little man in a black frock coat. And this is the third principal character of our story. Its function: perhaps to give Mr Al Denton his second chance."

Al Denton (Dan Duryea) is a drunken cowboy in the Old West who was once famed for his sharpshooting and reflexes. His insatiable desire for alcohol has now made him a humiliated, mocked and broken man. An enigmatic stranger by the name of Henry J Fate (Malcolm Atterbury) restores Al's dignity through supernatural sleight of hand but our troubled hero faces a severe test of nerve and confidence when an up and coming gunslinger called Grant (Doug McClure) arrives for a duel...

The first of Twilight Zone's western stories, Mr Denton on Doomsday is an above average drama boosted by the sympathetic performance of Dan Duryea as Denton. Duryea (who was apparently usually cast as villains) is especially strong in the scenes where he confesses that being the fastest draw in town - and so inevitably attracting constant challenges from the new kid on the block - is what drove him to drink in the first place. This life of violence and death has taken a heavy toll.

Look out for a wonderfully slimy turn by a young Martin Landau as a bully who delights in humiliating Al at the start of the story and also a baby faced Doug McClure in an early role as the sharpshooter intent on knocking Al off of his perch. While Mr Denton on Doomsday is not quite gold standard Twilight Zone the strong dialogue by Serling and sincere performances make it very worthwhile. Mr Denton on Doomsday is a successful first foray into the western genre for The Twilight Zone. You may guess the ending before we get there but this is a poignant tale with a good atmosphere and given a big boost by the cast. B

THE SIXTEEN-MILLIMETER SHRINE (Director: Mitchell Leisen, Writer: Rod Serling)

"Picture of a woman looking at a picture. Movie great of another time, once-brilliant star in a firmament no longer a part of the sky, eclipsed by the movement of earth and time. Barbara Jean Trenton, whose world is a projection room, whose dreams are made out of celluloid. Barbara Jean Trenton, struck down by hit-and-run years and lying on the unhappy pavement, trying desperately to get the license number of fleeting fame."

Barbara Jean Trenton (Ida Lupino) is an old movie star from the 1930s who now lives as a recluse in her mansion, idling her days away watching her old films with nostalgic bittersweet enchantment. Her agent Danny (Martin Balsam) must somehow get her to face up to reality and live for today - not yearn hopelessly for yesterday...

The Sixteen-Millimeter Shrine is a poignant episode about the passing of time and how this unavoidable part of human existence is harder for some than others. Barbara Jean was the talk of the town twenty-five years ago but growing older and seeing her star and beauty wane has not been easy. The fantastical ending doesn't make any sense but works in no small part thanks to the haunting music by Frank Waxman - which gives The Sixteen-Millimeter Shrine a dreamy atmosphere.

What lifts the story are the rich performances from Lupino and Martin Balsam, the pair given some good dialogue by Serling. Jerome Cowan of The Maltese Falcon makes a cameo as a former leading man of Barbara - the scene conveying everything about Barbara's character. She can barely face being in the same room with him because he simply reminds her that they are all older now. Not a great episode but the score and the performances are superb. This is sort of Sunset

Boulevard meets The Purple Rose of Cairo and a very dreamlike half hour of television. B-

WALKING DISTANCE (Director: Robert Stevens, Writer: Rod Serling)

"Martin Sloan, age thirty-six. Occupation: vice-president, ad agency, in charge of media. This is not just a Sunday drive for Martin Sloan. He perhaps doesn't know it at the time, but it's an exodus. Somewhere up the road he's looking for sanity. And somewhere up the road, he'll find something else."

Martin Sloan (Gig Young) is an unhappy executive suffering from a life crisis and dreaming of the innocent, carefree days of his childhood. One day, he leaves his car and decides to walk to the small town where he spent his youth. When he arrives Martin is shocked to discover that nothing seems to have changed at all...

Walking Distance is the first truly great Twilight Zone episode and one of the most affecting in the long history of the series. Serling taps into his own life, the stresses and strains of his workload and desire to return to a simpler way of life and the romanticised memories of childhood and youth. This is a wistful, nostalgic fantasy rather than overt science fiction, a touching story about the burdens of adulthood and altogether one of the most poignant ever written for the Twilight Zone.

Walking Distance was inspired by Rod Serling walking through the MGM set in the 1950s and being struck by how much it reminded him of the town he grew up in. It occurred to him how people have a longing to go home - but to the misty, romantic notion of home they remember from their childhood. A place you can never actually go back to (except of course in the Twilight Zone). It was a familiar Serling theme, a man having a personal crisis and yearning to escape from the dog eat dog modern world with all of its stresses and strains.

Serling's incredible workload often left him shattered and on the verge of a nervous breakdown himself and he incorporated this into several moving stories.

The central character here, Martin Sloan is overworked, stressed out and at the end of his tether. In an allusion to Alice in Wonderland (and maybe The Wizard of Oz too presumably) he abandons his car and heads down a quiet road on foot towards the small town he grew up in. Bernard Herrmann's beautiful score is a perfect backdrop for the moving scenes of Martin reconnecting with a world he thought was gone forever. The simple act of buying an ice cream in his old home town is wonderfully played. There is of course a bittersweet edge to the fantasy with Martin realising - as everyone must - that you can't go home again but Serling's meditation on this theme is consistently interesting and poignant. His closing narration is one of his most memorable. A classic Twilight Zone episode. A

ESCAPE CLAUSE (Director: Mitchell Leisen, Writer: Rod Serling)

"You're about to meet a hypochondriac. Witness Mr Walter Bedeker age forty-four. Afraid of the following: death, disease, other people, germs, draft, and everything else. He has one interest in life and that's Walter Bedeker. One preoccupation, the life and well-being of Walter Bedeker. One abiding concern about society, that if Walter Bedeker should die how will it survive without him?"

A hypochondriac named Walter Bedeker (David Wayne) makes a deal with the Devilish Mr Cadwallader (Thomas Gomez) for immortality in exchange for his soul. The escape clause? If Walter ever becomes weary of immortality a peaceful death will be his for the asking...

Escape Clause makes for a decent black comedy with David

Wayne enjoying himself as the misanthropic Walter - our anti-hero prone to increasingly self destructive behaviour as the burdens of immortality begin to hit home. The moral of the story is relatively simple - how can you truly appreciate life as a precious thing if nothing can harm you and you know it will last forever? - and while Escape Clause is Rod Serling coasting to an extent he wrings enough laughs and food for thought to make this one breeze past in likeable enough fashion.

This is a fairly entertaining little episode with lashings of black humour and a wonderful performance by David Wayne as the cantankerous Bedeker. His increasing boredom with immortality is fun as he becomes increasingly immoral and prone to doing things like throwing himself in front of a train! This an effective sequence with copious use of dry ice. While the budget for these shows is clearly not astronomical they are inventive in terms of their production. There's a nice twist in the tale here too. Escape Clause is decent fun on the whole but not one of the very best or most ambitious episodes in season one. B-

THE LONELY (Director: Jack Smight, Writer: Rod Serling)

"Witness if you will a dungeon, made out of mountains, salt flats and sand that stretch to infinity. The dungeon has an inmate: James A Corry. And this is his residence: a metal shack. An old touring car that squats in the sun and goes nowhere - for there is nowhere to go.

For the record let it be known that James A Corry is a convicted criminal placed in solitary confinement. Confinement in this case stretches as far as the eye can see, because this particular dungeon is on an asteroid nine million miles from the Earth. Now witness if you will a man's mind and body shrivelling in the sun, a man dying of loneliness."

In the year 2046, a convicted murderer named Corry (Jack Warden) is banished to live alone on a desert like asteroid for fifty years - though he seems a gentle soul and maintains that it was an act of self defence. When the supply ship from Earth arrives for a brief stop, the Captain ((John Dehner) has sympathy for the lonely plight of Corry and leaves him a lifelike female robot for company...

A classic episode, The Lonely is a haunting meditation on the effect isolation and alienation can have on the human spirit. Serling's thoughtful screenplay is done full justice by the inspired casting of Jack Warden as Corry and authentic location work that conveys the desperate circumstances of his punishment, sent to live on a world where he is the only inhabitant. Warden convincingly conveys the arc of Corry, appalled by the synthetic companion at first but then falling in love with "Alicia" because he has no one else to turn to. Jean Marsh gives a strong performance as Alicia and makes the ending all the more poignant.

The sun baked kooky Death Valley location really does give one the impression of a far distant world. Cory's isolation is starkly conveyed by his metal shack home - the only blip on a vast barren landscape. This is another rumination by Serling on the need for human contact and one of his best on this theme.

"Every morning when I get up I tell myself this is my last day of sanity. I can't stand this loneliness one more day, not one more day! I know when I can't keep my fingers still and the inside of my mouth feels like gunpowder and burnt copper. Down deep inside my gut I get an ache that's just pulling everything out. Then I force myself to hold on for one more day, just one more day. But I can't do that for another 46 years, Allenby. I'll go right out of my mind."

The Lonely is classic Twilight Zone. A-

TIME ENOUGH AT LAST (Director: John Brahm, Writer: Rod Serling)

"Witness Mr. Henry Bemis, a charter member in the fraternity of dreamers. A bookish little man whose passion is the printed page but who is conspired against by a bank president and a wife and a world full of tongue-cluckers and the unrelenting hands of a clock. But in just a moment Mr. Bemis will enter a world without bank presidents or wives or clocks or anything else. He'll have a world all to himself without anyone."

Henry Bemis (Burgess Meredith) is a short-sighted bank clerk and compulsive book worm. Henry is constantly frustrated by his lack of quality reading time but soon he might have all the time in the world...

This was based on a short story by Lynn Venable and expanded by Serling (while retaining the rather heartbreaking but delicious twist at the end). Burgess Meredith would star in four Twilight Zone episodes but this was by far the most famous and memorable. He makes Bemis a loveable misfit and an amusing and introspective man that we always feel sympathy for. One of the most fondly remembered stories in the history of the show, Time Enough at Last has one of the most famous (and heartbreaking) twist endings and a charming central performance by Twilight Zone regular Burgess Meredith as the weedy put upon Bemis.

The story switches from a domestic comic tale of a man who just can't stand up for himself to an apocalyptic last act and the set designs (on what was a limited budget) are nicely inventive. Memorable images include Bemis bouncing around in the bank vault he sneaks in to read in peace and the library steps that still somehow stand despite the destruction all around them. The actual steps used in the production were still standing from a set on the MGM backlot and wonderfully atmospheric. Jacqueline deWitt and Vaughn Taylor lend solid support as Henry's disapproving wife and Scrooge like boss respectively. Time Enough at Last is a justifiably famous episode. A-

PERCHANCE TO DREAM (Director: Robert Florey, Writer: Charles Beaumont)

"Twelve o'clock noon. An ordinary scene, an ordinary city. Lunchtime for thousands of ordinary people. To most of them, this hour will be a rest, a pleasant break in the day's routine. To most, but not all. To Edward Hall, time is an enemy, and the hour to come is a matter of life and death."

Edward Hall (Richard Conte) is a man with a cardiac condition who tells his psychiatrist Dr Rathmann (John Larch) that if he falls asleep he thinks he will die. The reason? He has been trapped in a recurring dream that always features a sultry carnival dancer named Maya (Suzanne Lloyd) trying to entice him into a funfair and onto a roller coaster with the intention of frightening him to death. If he goes asleep and returns to the dream he believes he will have a heart attack in his sleep. But staying awake forever will be an impossible strain on his heart too. What can he do?

Charles Beaumont's first Twilight Zone story is an engagingly strange fable with a neat premise (Edward must stay awake all the time or risk heart failure!) and makes the most of the recurring carnival nightmare with exotic dancer Maya (Suzanne Lloyd) forever trying to lure him into a funfair where the rides will surely be too much for his fragile heart. This is a highly inventive and energetic episode with a freaky creepy funfair carnival atmosphere and a breathless and perfect performance by Richard Conte as Hall. Conte was actually in The Godfather many years later. Beaumont's script is tightly conceived and presents the amusement park as a nightmare. He obviously had big issues with funfairs and dreams!

It's the surreal dreamlike atmosphere which sustains this

episode and holds your attention. As ever with The Twilight Zone the black and white photography enjoyably adds to the strange ambiance. You would not call Perchance To Dream a classic Twilight Zone episode but it is a unique and engagingly bonkers experience and certainly worthy of your time. This is a fun entry into the Twilight Zone for Charles Beaumont. B

JUDGMENT NIGHT (Director: John Brahm, Writer: Rod Serling)

"Her name is the S.S. Queen of Glasgow. Her registry: British. Gross tonnage: five thousand. Age: indeterminate. At this moment she's one day out of Liverpool, her destination New York. Duly recorded on this ship's log is the sailing time, course to destination, weather conditions, temperature, longitude and latitude. But what is never recorded in a log is the fear that washes over a deck like fog and ocean spray. Fear like the throbbing strokes of engine pistons, each like a heartbeat, parceling out every hour into breathless minutes of watching, waiting and dreading. For the year is 1942, and this particular ship has lost its convoy. It travels alone like an aged blind thing groping through the unfriendly dark, stalked by unseen periscopes of steel killers. Yes, the Queen of Glasgow is a frightened ship, and she carries with her a premonition of death."

The Queen of Glasgow is sailing from Liverpool to New York in 1942 and onboard is a German man named Carl Lanser (Nehemiah Persoff) who has absolutely no idea how he got on a British ship. But Lanser has a strange feeling that he knows the passengers and crew and has seen them before. He also has an overwhelming premonition that the ship is doomed and that something terrible will happen at exactly 1.15 am...

A recurring nightmare ghost story with a strong sense of atmosphere and some impressive sets (recycled from The Wreck of the Mary Deare), Judgment Night is a satisfying

chiller with an appropriately frazzled performance by
Nehemiah Persoff. Serling's clever script makes this a story
that one can return to even with knowledge of the twist at the
end and still find interesting - especially as we then piece the
clues together. The crew of the ship soon begin to become
suspicious of Lanser.

Viewers of this episode will note an early role for Avengers star
Patrick Macnee as the captain of the ship. Judgment Night is
an enjoyable and compelling episode and another strong story
for series one. The deja vu aspect to the story is something that
has been done to death by now in fantasy and science fiction
but it never feels too alarmingly rote or derivative here and the
episode has a nice sense of atmosphere. Look out for the way
some real U-boat footage is enjoyably incorporated into this
episode. B

AND WHEN THE SKY WAS OPENED (Director: Douglas Heyes, Writer: Richard Matheson)

"Her name: X-20. Her type: an experimental interceptor.
Recent history: a crash landing in the Mojave Desert after a
thirty-one hour flight nine hundred miles into space.
Incidental data: the ship, with the men who flew her,
disappeared from the radar screen for twenty-four hours. But
the shrouds that cover mysteries are not always made out of a
tarpaulin, as this man will soon find out on the other side of a
hospital door."

Three astronauts - Gart (Jim Hutton), Forbes (Rod Taylor)
and Harrington (Charles Aidmen) - return as heroes after the
first space expedition but back on Earth they begin to have an
overwhelming and unsettling feeling that they don't belong
there anymore. Very soon their existence begins to come under
threat...

Richard Matheson's first Twilight Zone screenplay (based on his short story Disappearing Act) makes for a superior episode with strong direction by Douglas Heyes. Heyes would return for further classic episodes (The After Hours, Eye of the Beholder and The Howling Man) and he builds a great deal of suspense and fear as the astronauts begin to be erased from history one by one. Loss of identity and memory is a theme the series would examine in later stories but And When the Sky Was Opened rates as highly as most of them.

Jim Hutton is sympathetic as the young central astronaut and Rod Taylor (of The Time Machine fame) and Charles Aidmen are believable as his colleagues. A memorable episode made all the more compelling by the uneasy sense of the inevitable that pervades the story. These men can't seem to escape from their mysterious fate and that is terrifying because the fate in question is essentially wiping them from existence! One might propose that a subtext of the story here is death - a fate that also erases all that one was. The fate of these astronauts is even worse than death though because because no one will remember they even existed in the first place. B+

WHAT YOU NEED (Director: Alvin Ganzer, Writer: Rod Serling)

"You're looking at Mr. Fred Renard, who carries on his shoulder a chip the size of the national debt. This is a sour man, a friendless man, a lonely man, a grasping, compulsive, nervous man. This is a man who has lived thirty-six undistinguished, meaningless, pointless, failure-laden years and who at this moment looks for an escape - any escape, any way, anything, anybody - to get out of the rut. And this little old man is just what Mr. Renard is waiting for."

Pedott (Ernest Truex) is a mysterious but kind hearted salesman who seems to know exactly what people will need in the future. However, an intimidating crook named Renard

(Steve Cochran) tries to exploit his ability...

What You Need is lighter episode that doesn't bear too much close inspection but the uncanny gifts of the salesman are used to nice effect by Serling's script and Ernest Truex gives a likeable performance as the wise old hustler. He's matched by Steve Cochran as the obnoxious and frightening Renard and the battle of wills between the two very different men moves the story along in generally agreeable fashion.

When the sour bully Renard notices the abilities of Pedott, he demands that he be given something that will help him too as he is something of a bitter loser in life. Pedott gives him a pair of scissors and Renard isn't too impressed. However, when he gets his tie caught in a lift the scissors save his life and he realises that Pedott has a truly remarkable ability. He goes back to the old man and keeps demanding more and more things. Pedott soon realises that he is going to have to come up with a plan to get this dangerous and immoral bully off his back and out of his life.

This is the sort of story that would outstay its welcome in a longer format but the brief running time of Twilight Zone (save for one later season as we shall see later) means that it never threatens your patience. The fantastical concept of the story has some nice little pay-offs and this is all agreeable enough. It probably won't lodge in the memory as one of the most memorable Twilight Zone episodes but you should have a decent enough time while you are watching. Far from a classic but a likeable enough episode. B-

THE FOUR OF US ARE DYING (Director: John Brahm, Writer: Rod Serling)

"His name is Arch Hammer. He's thirty-six years old. He's been a salesman, a dispatcher, a truck driver, a con man, a bookie, and a part-time bartender. This is a cheap man, a nickel and dime man, with a cheapness that goes past the suit and the shirt; a cheapness of mind, a cheapness of taste, a tawdry little shine on the seat of his conscience, and a darkroom squint at a world whose sunlight has never gotten through to him..."

A shady man named Arch Hammer (Robert Townes) can alter his appearance to mimic other people. As you might imagine this leads to all manner of complicated - and also dangerous - shenanigans. He checks into a motel and impersonates a trumpet player named Johnny (Ross Martin) to get Johnny's girlfriend Maggie (Beverly Garland) and then later a murdered gangster named Strerig (Phillip Pine) to exhort some money from the hood who thought he had killed Strerig. This is only the start of his face changing capers though and as this is the Twilight Zone Hammer is probably going to get more than he bargained for...

An interesting episode (taken from an unpublished story by George Clayton Johnson), The Four of Us Are Dying doesn't threaten the Twilight Zone top table but still has much going for it. Hammer's ability is conveyed with some clever optical effects and directorial sleight of hand and the smoke hazed jazz world of gangsters and night strobed alleyways gives The Four of Us Are Dying a strong sense of atmosphere. Townes is an interesting presence as Hammer and Jerry Goldsmith's score makes a fine backdrop to the action. You might describe this as an inventive second tier Twilight Zone entry.

There's a risk here that the concept is more interesting than the story (and so doesn't do the concept full justice) but this is a fairly compelling experience once the plot gets going and it's all engaging enough. Despite the absurd premise, this is played straight and beautifully directed with some excellent performances. Love the shot of Hammer shaving early on where his face changes twice in the mirror. The Four of Us Are Dying is no classic but it is clever and competent. B-

THIRD FROM THE SUN (Director: Richard L Bare, Writer: Rod Serling)

"Quitting time at the plant. Time for supper now. Time for families. Time for a cool drink on a porch. Time for the quiet rustle of leaf-laden trees that screen out the moon. And underneath it all, behind the eyes of the men, hanging invisible over the summer night, is a horror without words. For this is the stillness before storm. This is the eve of the end."

Fearful of an impending nuclear war, scientist William Sturka (Fritz Weaver) plans to steal a secret government flying saucer so his family can escape into space. The only problem is the obstinately suspicious government agent named Carling (Harry Andrews)...

A great episode, Third from the Sun has a memorable twist at the end but is most successful in building suspense as Sturka's painstaking plans to steal the saucer craft are threatened by the sweaty and forever prying attentions of Carling. Andrews and Weaver are both superb in their roles with good support by Joe Maross as Sturka's co-conspirator Jerry. The extended card game sequence where Andrews arrives at the house is wonderfully tense.

The flying saucer is fun in this story too and was used in Forbidden Planet. Third from the Sun works really well because of the tension and paranoia it laces into the story and it helps of course that this is all played by a terrific cast. This is a really good episode and the sort of thing that Serling and The Twilight Zone always did so well.

One thing that really helps this episode is that we are rooting for the central characters to escape because we know they've spent months planning their mission. Because we are invested in the plight of these characters this means Carling works even better as a villain. A-

I SHOT AN ARROW INTO THE AIR
(Director: Stuart Rosenberg, Writer: Rod Serling)

"Her name is the Arrow One. She represents four and a half years of planning, preparation and training, and a thousand years of science and mathematics and the projected dreams and hopes of not only a nation but a world. She is the first manned aircraft into space. And this is the countdown, the last five seconds before man shot an arrow into the air."

Three astronauts are stranded on rocky asteroid with a limited supply of water. Colonel Donlin (Edward Binns) soon has his hands full though with the scheming and potentially mutinous Corey (Dewey Martin)...

I Shot an Arrow into the Air was written by Rod Serling from an idea by Madelon Champion. Champion suggested the idea for the story to Serling during a conversation and was paid $500 for it. Although Serling always encouraged ideas and screenplays from "outsiders" this was the only time he ever deemed one of them interesting enough to use. I Shot an Arrow into the Air is best remembered for the twist ending (which you may well see coming anyway - thus potentially negating its impact) and probably deserves a slightly better reputation than it has in the Twilight Zone pantheon.

Serling's extra narration over the third act seems somewhat gratuitous (Serling does some narration during the episode over rocky desert vistas in addition to his usual vocal duties at the beginning and end) and the twist unavoidably makes the characters look rather stupid in retrospect but the story is always sufficiently gripping and Dewey Martin makes a good stock Twilight Zone villain as the increasingly unhinged Corey. I'm always a sucker for these types of stories where they have astronauts trapped somewhere strange and getting on each other's nerves.

The use of Death Valley for the location gives this an authentically weird and desolate atmosphere and all in all it's a solid enough Twilight Zone. You might even say that this is an underrated Twilight Zone episode. It isn't perfect by any means but it is competent and engaging enough for what it is. This episode - on a science level - doesn't make much sense when you think about it afterwards but it is absorbing. B

THE HITCH-HIKER (Director: Alvin Ganzer, Writer: Rod Serling)

"Her name is Nan Adams. She's twenty-seven years old. Her occupation: buyer at a New York department store, at present on vacation, driving cross-country to Los Angeles, California, from Manhattan. Minor incident on Highway 11 in Pennsylvania, perhaps to be filed away under accidents you walk away from. But from this moment on, Nan Adams's companion on a trip to California will be terror; her route - fear; her destination - quite unknown."

Nan Adams (Inga Stevens) is a young woman on a long car journey. After a tyre blows out, she keeps on seeing a strange hitch-hiker (Leonard Strong) by the road who seems to be beckoning her to follow him. No matter how far she drives he keeps appearing again. Who is he and what does he want?

This is another memorable episode in the mostly classic first season of The Twilight Zone. A haunting atmosphere is superbly maintained throughout and takes us to a touching climax. While the premise might feel familiar to modern viewers this is a classic rendering of an oft riffed fantasy staple. Inga Stevens makes a fine confused heroine and Leonard Strong is well cast as the shabby and increasingly ominous hitch-hiker.

At its best this episode has some of the ambience of weird vintage 60s horror movies like Carnival of Souls. The narration by the heroine is a trifle purple but enjoyable enough and the strange baffling aura of mystery which pervades the story is strong and vivid. I think The Hitch-Hiker is possibly a trifle overrated in Twilight Zone retrospectives but I certainly wouldn't dispute that it is a very interesting and effective episode. The road movie quality (a spooky road movie at that!) to this story is certainly enjoyable too. Look out for the great tense sequence where Nan's car stalls on some railway tracks. B+

THE FEVER (Director: Robert Florey, Writer: Rod Serling)

"Mr and Mrs Franklin Gibbs, three days and two nights, all expenses paid, at a Las Vegas hotel, won by virtue of Mrs Gibbs's knack with a phrase. But unbeknownst to either Mr. or Mrs Gibbs is the fact that there's a prize in their package neither expected nor bargained for. In just a moment one of them will succumb to an illness worse than any virus can produce, a most inoperative, deadly, life-shattering affliction known as the fever."

The tight fisted Scrooge like Franklin Gibbs (Everett Sloane) is not terribly thrilled when his wife Flora (Viva Janis) wins a holiday in Las Vegas. He hates gambling - although Flora is rather excited by the holiday. Anyway, when a drunk thrusts a silver dollar in his hand and makes him activate a one-armed bandit slot machine, Gibbs has a big win. He then keeps hearing the slot machine call out his name and is irresistibly drawn to the one-armed bandit. His rationale is that the winnings are tainted money so he may as well get rid of it by putting it back in the machine. Gibbs is soon hopelessly addicted to the slot machine and spends all hours of the day there losing all of their money in a frantic obsessed sweaty haze. Why does it have such power over him?

A lighter episode and a middle-ranking one by the high

standards of season one but The Fever is watchable enough thanks mainly to Everett Sloane's frazzled performance as Franklin - a man who begins the story prim and proper and then gradually loses his mind as his gambling obsession consumes him. The casino scenes are a lot of fun here and Serling seems to be enjoying himself, especially in the scenes he includes where the slot machine takes on a life of its own and seems to call out to Franklin. The Fever is a fun little episode but not one of the best in season one.

This episode was apparently inspired by Rod Serling visiting Las Vegas with his wife. Maybe he got hooked on a slot machine himself and decided to write a story about it? The Fever is fairly forgettable in the long run and doesn't hold a candle to the best Twilight Zone episodes but it's engaging and amusing enough for what it is. This is definitely though one of those Twilight Zones that would have got tiresome in an hour long format. The concept is pretty slight but thankfully doesn't outstay its welcome in the shorter format. B-

THE LAST FLIGHT (Director: William Claxton, Writer: Richard Matheson)

"Witness Flight Lieutenant William Terrance Decker, Royal Flying Corps, returning from a patrol somewhere over France. The year is 1917. The problem is that the Lieutenant is hopelessly lost. Lieutenant Decker will soon discover that a man can be lost not only in terms of maps and miles, but also in time, and time in this case can be measured in eternities."

A British World War I pilot named Lt William Terrence Decker (Kenneth Haigh) lands on an air base in France and is astonished when the American commanders there tell him the year is 1959. It appears Decker has jumped into the future...

This is a good time travel episode with a layered and intelligent script and good location work at a real air base (not to mention use of an authentic 1918 Nieport biplane). Kenneth Haigh gives a credible performance as the British pilot who has somehow escaped from his own time and the story arc of Decker having the chance to rewrite history gives the story both impetus and a satisfying last act. The supporting cast are believable and Serling wrings full value out of the outlandish premise.

The characters are pretty good in The Last Flight and behave in a realistic way despite the fantastical premise. Note how Decker is somewhat suspicious of the Americans at first and bemused at how advanced they are. He comes from a time when America was largely isolationist in nature and didn't play a major role in world affairs. One wouldn't call The Last Flight one of the very best Twilight Zone episodes but it's strong and well made all the same and manages to pack a lot of story into its thirty minutes without the plot ever feeling clunky or overstuffed. This was the first completely non-Rod Serling script to go into production and it's a very strong one. It's very talky at times but the actors handle this well. B+

THE PURPLE TESTAMENT (Director: Richard L Bare, Writer: Rod Serling)

"Infantry platoon, U.S. Army, Phillipine Islands, 1945. These are the faces of the young men who fight. As if some omniscient painter had mixed a tube of oils that were at one time earth brown, dust gray, blood red, beard black, and fear - yellow white, and these men were the models. For this is the province of combat and these are the faces of war."

In the war torn Far East of World War 2, Lt Fitzgerald (William Reynolds) always notices a strange eerie glow in the face of the soldier in his platoon who is destined to die next...

Serling taps into his own World War 2 experiences for this poignant story. The limited budget places some unavoidable constraints on the production with a stagebound hokey jungle atmosphere but the acting is solid and the premise is haunting - especially the spooky light on the faces of the doomed men. Soldiers in World War 2 really did look into the faces of friends knowing that it might be the last time they ever saw them alive.

One might argue that The Purple Testament - the premonition plot notwithstanding - feels rather generic with its World War 2 setting and you could say it's a little dull compared to more overtly fantastical episodes of this show. The ending is not exactly impossible to predict. You just KNOW where this story is going to end up. These quibbles aside though it's decent enough if never what you would describe as the most gripping or memorable episode of this show. This is lesser episode in the excellent season one but a reasonably solid one by most standards nonetheless. The glow on the doomed soldier's faces was achieved by overexposing the film and is rather eerie. B-

ELEGY (Director: Douglas Heyes, Writer: Charles Beaumont)

"The time is the day after tomorrow. The place: a far corner of the universe. The cast of characters: three men lost amongst the stars, three men sharing the common urgency of all men lost - they're looking for home. And in a moment they'll find home, not a home that is a place to be seen but a strange, unexplainable experience to be felt."

In the year 2185, astronauts Kurt Meyers (Jeff Morrow), Captain James Webber (Kevin Hagen), and Peter Kirby (Don Dubbins), run out of fuel and set down on an asteroid where they are perplexed to find very Earthlike conditions. More puzzling than that though is the fact that the people they find are all frozen to the spot as if they are statues. A marching band, violinists, people playing cards, even a beauty contest. Everyone frozen. The only person who does move and speak to them is a jovial old man named Jeremy (Cecil Kellaway). What is this place and who is the old man?

Elegy is rather morbid but benefits from the sprightly performance of Kellaway and the central mystery is very Twilight Zone. Frozen people/time capers were done to death in the end by this series, The Outer Limits and things like Star Trek but one must presume it was a tad more novel here in 1960. The atmosphere of this story is good and one is initially intrigued by the predicament of the central characters and the strange place they find themselves in. This reminded me somewhat of Ray Bradbury's The Martian Chronicles.

Though an interesting episode, Elegy - frustratingly - doesn't quite become as good as you want it to be. It wrings a decent amount of watchability from the premise though with the bric a brac of a small town in perfect stillness. A strange old man named Jeremy is the only person there able to move and speak and he will provide the resolution to the mystery. The Twilight Zone would return to the 'frozen in time premise' in future shows and while Elegy is no classic it is a fair test run for this recurring plot device.

While the concept of this episode is intriguing the actual episode itself never threatens to become especially memorable and so doesn't do the concept justice. One obvious flaw here is that you can plainly see the actors playing the frozen people wobbling and moving at times. Elegy is an episode that probably should have been a lot better than it actually turned to be. For some reason it never satisfies or hits the mark in the way it should. An ok episode but no great shakes. B-

MIRROR IMAGE (Director: John Brahm, Writer: Rod Serling)

"Millicent Barnes, age twenty-five, young woman waiting for a bus on a rainy November night. Not a very imaginative type is

Miss Barnes, not given to undue anxiety or fears, or for that matter even the most temporal flights of fancy. Like most young career women, she has a generic classification as a, quote, girl with a head on her shoulders, end of quote. All of which is mentioned now because in just a moment the head on Miss Barnes's shoulders will be put to a test. Circumstances will assault her sense of reality and a chain of nightmares will put her sanity on a block. Millicent Barnes, who in one minute will wonder is she's going mad."

While waiting for a bus at the lonely bus station on a rainy night, Millicent Barnes (Vera Miles) has a most unsettling time with an apparent duplicate of herself...

Mirror Image is an enjoyable little episode with good use made of the restrictive bus station setting and some eerie touches that engage the viewer and make the story consistently entertaining and compelling. Rod Serling got the idea for Mirror Image when he spotted someone at an airport who was the exact same height as him with identical clothes and the same briefcase. He thought about how creepy it would be if the person turned around and it was him!

The story here feels like a twist on Anthony Armstrong's novel The Strange Case of Mr Pelham (the book inspiring an episode of Alfred Hitchcock Presents and later adapted into an excellent film starring Roger Moore). Vera Miles is nicely cast as the increasingly bemused heroine in Mirror Image and makes a good window through which the story is told. The threat to one's sense of identity is a frequent trope for stories through the history of The Twilight Zone and Mirror Image is clearly one of the superior examples of this familiar fantasy premise. The constrictive bus station location is a suitably strange backdrop for the story.

Anyone who has ever waited for a late night bus or train (and most of us have had this experience at some time or other) will testify that public transport stations can sometimes be creepy and lonely places at night. Mirror Image enjoyably taps into that aura. Good support here too by Martin Milner as Paul Grinstead, an amiable businessman also waiting for a bus who is sympathetic to Millicent's plight and tries to help her. B+

THE MONSTERS ARE DUE ON MAPLE STREET (Director: Ronald Winston, Writer: Rod Serling)

"Maple Street, U.S.A. Late summer. A tree-lined little world of front porch gliders, barbecues, the laughter of children, and the bell of an ice-cream vendor. At the sound of the roar and the flash of light, it will be precisely 6:43pm on Maple Street. This is Maple Street on a late Saturday afternoon. Maple Street, in the last calm and reflective moment before the monsters came."

The residents of a usually peaceful and pleasant street descend into paranoia and witch hunts after a series of strange events which they suspect might involve aliens. Is one of them not who they appear to be?

The Monsters Are Due on Maple Street is a Rod Serling meditation on the need to remain civilised. The ensemble of actors work well together as tempers fray and while the science fiction coda is a little hokey it is a lot of fun in the best Twilight Zone tradition. The Monsters Are Due on Maple Street is based around one of Serling's frequent themes of how humanity needs to remain decent and kind if it is to have any future. Civilisation is a fragile thing. Could you count on your neighbour in a real crisis or would they simply be out for themselves and have no hesitation in turning on you? These are rich themes for a Twilight Zone story and work well in The Monsters Are Due on Maple Street.

This is enjoyably reminiscent of old science fiction classics like Invasion of the Body Snatchers and Invaders From Mars although the real monsters are of course ourselves rather than

aliens. Very Cold War paranoia - something that The Twilight
Zone and many science fiction writers tapped into at the time.
There is of course a less than veiled subtext of McCarthyism in
the story too with the people of Maple Street whipping
themselves up into a frenzy and panic - that may or may not be
completely misplaced - and looking for someone to blame. It's
a clever rumination on paranoia and the nature of fear and
how we always look for scapegoats when something goes
wrong.

Claude Atkins is solid as the central character Steve Brand.
Brand wants to go into town but is warned that the power
shortage is meant to isolate and contain the neighbourhood. It
might be dangerous to leave. He isn't convinced though and
not impressed by the increasing paranoia. The story here has
plenty to say about the inability of people to trust outsiders
and think the worst of them. These all, sadly, remain timely
themes. The atmosphere is this story is generated by the way
electrical malfunctions signify something is wrong or
unfathomable forces are at play. It's a device that everything
from Close Encounters to Stranger Things has used in the
decades that followed Maple Street's transmission. The
Monsters are Due On Maple Street is a justifiably famous
episode and one that leaves plenty of food for thought. B+

A WORLD OF DIFFERENCE (Director: Ted Post, Writer: Richard Matheson)

"You're looking at a tableau of reality, things of substance, of
physical material: a desk, a window, a light. These things exist
and have dimension. Now this is Arthur Curtis, age thirty-six,
who also is real. He has flesh and blood, muscle and mind. But
in just a moment we will see how thin a line separates that
which we assume to be real with that manufactured inside of a
mind."

A man named Arthur Curtis (Howard Duff) is baffled when his

life and very identity is suggested to be merely a work of fiction...

An enjoyably twisty episode from the pen of Richard Matheson with an irresistible opening gambit - a man is in his office at work and it suddenly becomes a film set with everyone treating him as if he is an actor playing a part! They tell Arthur that he is really a drunken actor named Jerry Raigan and that "Arthur Curtis" is just a character he is playing in a film! Arthur is adamant that this is not the case though. He really is a businessman named Arthur Curtis. Curtis must turn detective to establish his own existence or his very sanity may be at risk.

This is the sort of story the Twilight Zone always did well and another Twilight Zone story which uses the loss of identity as a concept. A World of Difference is an enjoyable little episode which takes great pleasure in pulling the rug from the audience and its long suffering central character. Duff is perfectly fine as the baffled lead and Matheson's script gives the episode a very firm foundation from which to tell a generally entertaining and clever yarn. You wouldn't say this was an out and out classic but it is definitely worth watching during a Twilight Zone marathon. The concept is a lot of fun and hooks the viewer in right from the start. A clever and enjoyable episode on the whole. B

LONG LIVE WALTER JAMESON (Director: Tony Leader, Writer: Charles Beaumont)

"You're looking at Act One, Scene One, of a nightmare, one not restricted to witching hours or dark, rainswept nights. Professor Walter Jameson, popular beyond words, who talks of the past as if it were the present, who conjures up the dead as if they were alive. In the view of this man, Professor Samuel Kittridge, Walter Jameson has access to knowledge that couldn't come out of a volume of history, but rather from a book on black magic, which is to say that this nightmare begins at noon."

Professor Samuel Kittridge (Edgar Stehli) is very uneasy about Walter Jameson (Kevin McCarthy) - a colleague at work who is engaged to his daughter Susanna Kittridge (Dody Heath). Jameson never seems to age and has knowledge of American Civil War history not to be found in any text book. What is his secret?

This is another classic episode for Twilight Zone's mostly wonderful first year. This is a talky episode but a very compelling one with the ever dependable Kevin McCarthy (best known perhaps for Invasion of the Body Snatchers) perfectly cast as the mysterious Jameson. The story moves to a chilling conclusion and draws the viewer in more and more as we reach the final act. Long Live Walter Jameson is an effective tale of how immortality might not be attractive as it seems. Not only would you constantly have to experience those you care about dying but you would also find that life had to be lived on certain constrictive terms.

Jameson is a man who has to be careful of how much of himself he exposes to the world at large for fear of his secret becoming known. He has to blend into the background as much as he can and so his life is constrained and compromised. Would immortality be a gift or a curse? Long Live Walter Jameson suggests the latter in this chilling and absorbing yarn. This episode is highly recommended and definitely a contender for the Twilight Zone top table. Long Live Walter Jameson is built around a long conversation between Jameson and Kittridge and a fascinating and absorbing episode with elements of horror.

Be careful what you wish for is the message of the story and the wonderful Charles Beaumont takes the premise to its logical and horrible conclusion. A-

PEOPLE ARE ALIKE ALL OVER
(Director: Mitchell Leisen, Writer: Rod Serling)

"You're looking at a species of flimsy little two-legged animal with extremely small heads whose name is man. Warren Marcusson, age thirty-five. Samuel A. Conrad, age thirty-one. They're taking a highway into space, Man unshackling himself and sending his tiny, groping fingers up into the unknown. Their destination is Mars, and in just a moment we'll land there with them...."

Astronaut Mark Marcusson (Paul Comi) and scientist Sam Conrad (Roddy McDowall) crash land on the planet Mars and are spooked when something begins tapping on the hull of the downed spacecraft. Will the Martians be friendly?

An enjoyable episode that feels over familiar at times (we've already had crash landings on distant worlds more than once and we are only in season one!) but People Are Alike All Over works thanks to the memorable twist ending and the always watchable Roddy McDowall. McDowall is believably terrified when he is left alone and starts to hear noises coming from outside the downed spaceship.

The production design here is enjoyably hokey and very 1950s sci-fi at times. There are some very nice sci-fi images in this episode and the dated nature of the ships and costumes has a lot of charm today. The Martian landscapes came from the famed movie Forbiden Planet. This episode was adapted from a story by Paul Fairman called Brothers Beyond the Void. Serling apparently changed the story so that the weaker and more pessimistic Conrad became the central character. It's an idea that works very well. It would certainly be a shame too to have Roddy McDowall in a Twilight Zone and not make him the lead!

This episode has some thematic similarities to the classic later episode To Serve Man. In that episode, just as in People Are Alike All Over, the human race turns out to be insignificant and not as clever as they assumed in the wider context of an indifferent universe and other civilisations. I suppose you could probably describe that theme as rather Lovecraftian! I love the opening shot of the two looking out at their rocket ship on Earth. This is a very nicely done and anticipates what will happen later on. B+

EXECUTION (Director: David Orrick McDearmon, Writer: Rod Serling)

"Commonplace, if somewhat grim, unsocial event known as a necktie party, the guest of dishonor a cowboy named Joe Caswell, just a moment away from a rope, a short dance several feet off the ground, and then the dark eternity of all evil men. Mr Joe Caswell, who, when the good Lord passed out a conscience, a heart, a feeling for fellow men, must have been out for a beer and missed out. Mr Joe Caswell, in the last quiet moment of a violent life."

A dangerous criminal named Joe Carswell (Albert Salmi) vanishes in 1880 as he is about to be hung and is transported to the present day in the laboratory of Professor Sean Mannion (Russell Johnson). Mannion has used time travel to save Carswell's life but he soon begins to suspect that maybe that wasn't the most brilliant idea in the world...

Despite the interesting premise and the always dependable presence of Albert Salmi, this feels like the first misfire of season one and becomes more unsatisfying as it progresses - despite the symmetry of the resolution. The lab of Professor Mannion is never that convincing and makes the episode feel sillier than it needed to feel considering the weighty themes of justice and capital punishment. The story is really about the inevitability of fate and rehabilitation of criminals is another obvious theme here.

Carswell is pretty much beyond saving. He'd stab you in the back even if you were nice to him! The idea of a man from 1880 encountering the present day (1960 in this case) is fun on paper but doesn't really translate to a fun viewing experience here. It's quite a dull episode ultimately and never really grabs you in the way that the very best Twilight Zone episodes do. The ending is somewhat predictable too so leaves you feeling unsatisfied (though one might argue that it was the ONLY ending they could have gone for). This episode is a nice idea on paper but the (ahem) execution here doesn't quite work. C+

THE BIG TALL WISH (Director: Ron Winston, Writer: Rod Serling)

"In this corner of the universe, a prizefighter named Bolie Jackson, one hundred eighty-three pounds and an hour and a half away from a comeback at St. Nick's Arena. Mr.Bolie Jackson, who by the standards of his profession is an ageing, over-the-hill relic of what was, and who now sees a reflection of a man who has left too many pieces of his youth in too many stadiums for too many years before too many screaming people. Mr Bolie Jackson, who might do well to look for some gentle magic in the hard-surfaced glass that stares back at him."

Fading boxer Bolie Jackson (Ivan Dixon) is aided by a magical wish made by a boy named Henry (Steven Perry). However, a belief in magic will be required if the wish is to come true..

A Rod Serling penned boxing themed episode sounds like a can't miss but The Big Tall Wish is a strangely forgettable and sentimental episode that gains most of its watchability from the excellent work by the all black cast (which was obviously something of a rarity at the time). It's pleasant enough but never as magical or moving as Serling strives for it to be and so consequently A Big Tall Wish can't help coming across as, well, rather dull in the end. This is not one of those episodes that you'll find yourself rushing back to in Twilight Zone marathons. Given a choice there are countless Twilight Zone episodes you'd rather be watching again than The Big Tall Wish.

This is a whimsical but sometimes downbeat drama and it never really lives up to the sum of its parts. It's definitely not one of Serling's best scripts. The Big Tall Wish is ok but the story leans towards cliche and never becomes terribly interesting or engaging. I personally just never become immersed in this story much. Interesting trivia - the lead role in The Big Tall Wish was supposed to be played by the great real life boxer (and actor) Archie Moore but that casting obviously never transpired in the end. Ivan Dixon is very good though as Moore's replacement. C+

A NICE PLACE TO VISIT (Director: John Brahm, Writer: Charles Beaumont)

"Portrait of a man at work, the only work he's ever done, the only work he knows. His name is Henry Francis Valentine but he calls himself Rocky, because that's the way his life has been - rocky and perilous and uphill at a dead run all the way. He's tired now, tired of running or wanting, of waiting for the breaks that come to others but never to him, never to Rocky Valentine. A scared, angry little man. He thinks it's all over now but he's wrong. For Rocky Valentine, it's just the beginning."

A sleazy low-life criminal named Rocky Valentine (Larry Blyden) has all of his wishes granted by the mysterious Pip (Sebastian Cabot). Pip claims to be the guardian angel of wishes. But can he be trusted?

A Nice Place to Visit is not a classic but it's pretty good fun all the same with a nice twist in the tale. Larry Blyden is not the most convincing hood in the world (in fact, his performance is pretty terrible but then maybe he was just asked to play it broad?) but his somewhat over the top approach works in the context of the cartoon gangster world depicted in the story and Sebastian Cabot is enjoyable as Rocky's mysterious guardian. It's best to think of this as a more comic episode of The Twilight Zone and in that context it's actually not that bad at all and ambles along in fairly engaging fashion.

The twist is not impossible to see coming but the story does have a classic Twilight Zone quality in that you should be careful what you wish for. If you were literally given anything you wanted (as Rocky does in A Nice Place To Visit) wouldn't life sort of lose its meaning and any sense of purpose? You would be left with nothing to aim for and have no motivation to improve yourself as a person. If you can get past the broad performance of the lead actor this is worth a watch but don't expect it to be a classic because it plainly isn't. A Nice Place to Visit is a modestly amusing little episode but not much more than that. Trivia - the part of Rocky Valentine was apparently written with Mickey Rooney in mind. He was obviously unavailable though. B-

NIGHTMARE AS A CHILD (Director: Alvin Ganzer, Writer: Rod Serling)

"Month of November, hot chocolate, and a small cameo of a child's face, imperfect only in its solemnity. And these are the improbable ingredients to a human emotion, an emotion, say, like fear. But in a moment this woman, Helen Foley, will realize fear. She will understand what are the properties of terror. A little girl will lead her by the hand and walk with her into a nightmare."

A teacher named Helen Foley (Janice Rule) has an unforgettable encounter with a little girl called Markie (Terry

Burnham) in her apartment building. Markie seems to have intimate knowledge of Helen's past and seems determined to remind her of something that happened a long time ago...

Nightmare as a Child is something of a slow burn but becomes quite touching in the last act - even though you will probably guess where we are heading long before we actually get there. The unlocking of a childhood memory to solve a crime is not the most original premise but Nightmare As A Child has enough atmosphere and savvy to make it work relatively well here. Flaws in this episode are that the lead actors (including the child) are not brilliant and the direction is a little on the flat side. This doesn't have the style of the best Twilight Zone episodes.

The actual story is interesting enough though and quite a spooky aura is generated. While you wouldn't say that Nightmare as a Child is a classic episode you will become invested enough to want to see it through to the end. This is definitely worth a watch but you certainly wouldn't place it up there with the very best episodes of season one. Nightmare as a Child is an interesting episode but not a great one. The main flaw is that Janice Rule is never as sympathetic as the story suggests she should be. The actual mystery though is generally fine and one that somewhat mitigates the flaws in the cast and direction. B

A STOP AT WILLOUGHBY (Director: Robert Parrish, Writer: Rod Serling)

"This is Gart Williams, age thirty-eight, a man protected by a suit of armor all held together by one bolt. Just a moment ago, someone removed the bolt, and Mr Williams's protection fell away from him and left him a naked target. He's been cannonaded this afternoon by all the enemies of his life. His insecurity has shelled him, his sensitivity has straddled him with humiliation, his deep-rooted disquiet about his own worth has zeroed in on him, landed on target, and blown him apart. Mr Gart Williams, ad agency exec, who in just a moment will move into the Twilight Zone, in a desperate search for survival."

Gart Williams (James Daly) is a stressed executive who hates the modern world and is on the verge of a nervous breakdown. When he falls asleep on the train he awakes in the beautiful and anachronistic town of Willoughby...

One of the greatest of all Twilight Zone episodes, A Stop at Willoughby taps into one of Serling's most recurring themes: the yearning to find some escape from the pressures of the modern world and reality as a whole. Who hasn't dreamed of escaping from the rat race and experiencing a simpler way of life? Rod Serling definitely did. Willoughby feels like a place from another century and - unlike the modern world - Gart is always appreciated by everyone there, the pace of life blissfully unhurried. Everyone would surely like to have their own Willoughby to go and escape into.

James Daly is excellent as the lead here and draws our sympathy. Gart's boss Mr Misrell (Howard Smith) is a humourless bully and his wife Jane (Patricia Donahue) is a nagging shrew who loathes her husband for his lack of ambition and barely hides her contempt for him. The town of Willoughby by the way was an MGM set built for a film called Meet Me in St Louis. It makes a nice backdrop to the story. It's shot in a dreamy fashion and looks like something out of Huckleberry Finn.

A Stop at Willoughby is a great episode with a moving and haunting finale. This is like a companion piece to Walking Distance and once again incredibly moving and genuine because it feels like Serling is writing about himself. This is one of the great Twilight Zones of this or any other season. A

THE CHASER (Director: Dougls Heyes, Writer: Robert Presnell Jr)

"Mr Roger Shackleforth. Age: youthful twenties. Occupation: being in love. Not just in love, but madly, passionately, illogically, miserably, all-consumingly in love, with a young woman named Leila who has a vague recollection of his face and even less than a passing interest. In a moment you'll see a switch, because Mr Roger Shackleforth, the young gentleman so much in love, will take a short but very meaningful journey into the Twilight Zone."

Roger Shackleworth (George Grizzard) is in love with neighbour Leila (Patricia Barry) but she is indifferent to him and so visits Professor Deamon (John McIntire) to get a love potion. This being he Twilight Zone you should - as ever - be careful what you wish for...

A much lighter, throwaway episode, The Chaser feels weak compared to much of the other fare on offer in season one but the cast is good and - while predictable - the arc of the story is fun. Deamon's library is nicely designed with some surreal flourishes. This tale was enduring enough to feature again in Tales from the Crypt in the 1990s. George Grizzard is good here and this would not be his last visit to the Twilight Zone. While you've seen variations of this story before (and since!) it works well enough.

Roger is delighted when the potion makes the object of his desire fall in love with him but that love soon becomes constrictive and annoying. The potion works like a charm and Leila is soon absolutely besotted with Roger. However, her constant devotion and cloying reluctance to be apart from him even for a second soon becomes suffocating and unbearable. Roger must go back to Deamon and see if there is another potion that can provide a solution to this problem. The Chaser passes the time and is pleasant enough for what it is but all the same this is probably not a Twilight Zone episode you'll find yourself rushing back to in a hurry once you've seen it. It's a middling affair really. It's not bad but it's not terribly memorable either. B-

A PASSAGE FOR TRUMPET (Director: Don Medford, Writer: Rod Serling)

"Joey Crown, musician with an odd, intense face, whose life is a quest for impossible things like flowers in concrete or like trying to pluck a note of music out of the air and put it under glass to treasure. Joey Crown, musician with an odd, intense face, who in a moment will try to leave the Earth and discover the middle ground - the place we call the Twilight Zone."

A lonely, down at heel and drunken musician named Joey Crown (Jack Klugman) decides to end it all but then encounters an angel called Gabe (John Anderson)...

An unashamedly sentimental but touching episode that marks the first of Jack Klugman's appearances in The Twilight Zone. Klugman was never less than superb in the series and his performance here is typically powerful and committed. The story has a strong jazzy atmosphere and a rich surreal atmosphere when Joey realise that only Gabe can see him. The story here is pretty familiar (Joey thinks he isn't important and his life has been wasted but he learns that even the most seemingly ordinary people are important and special - basically It's a Wonderful Life all over again) but it is very touching and it helps of course to have Klugman as the lead. His mere presence makes the episode more compelling.

There's not an awful lot to dislike about A Passage for Trumpet. It's just a nice little gentler Twilight Zone episode that is trying to warm the heart rather than scare you and in this aim it succeeds very nicely. This is a moving episode with the first of Jack Klugman's wonderful Twilight Zone contributions. The monologues that Serling gives Klugman would have seemed overwritten in the hands of a lesser actor but they work beautifully here. B+

MR BEVIS (Director: William Ashner, Writer: Rod Serling)

"In the parlance of the twentieth century, this is an oddball. His name is James BW Bevis, and his tastes lean toward stuffed animals, zither music, professional football, Charles Dickens, moose heads, carnivals, dogs, children, and young ladies. Mr Bevis is accident prone, a little vague, a little discombobulated, with a life that possesses all the security of a floating crap game. But this can be said of our Mr Bevis: without him, without his warmth, without his kindness, the world would be a considerably poorer place, albeit perhaps a little saner. Should it not be obvious by now, James BW Bevis is a fixture in his own private, optimistic, hopeful little world, a world which has long ceased being surprised by him. James BW Bevis, on whom Dame Fortune will shortly turn her back, but not before she gives him a paste in the mouth. Mr James BW Bevis, just one block away from the Twilight Zone."

The eccentric Mr Bevis (Orson Bean) suffers a run of misfortune and is visited by a guardian angel (Henry Jones) - who teaches him that happiness is about being true to yourself and not about money and material possessions...

The first truly awful episode in series one, Mr Bevis is a comic misfire that feels out of place in The Twilight Zone. This was conceived as the pilot for a possible stand alone show with no lesser figure than Burgess Meredith as the lead but Meredith, wisely perhaps, passed on the offer. One can't really imagine that the adventures of Mr Bevis would have sustained much interest for viewers as getting through this single episode is enough of a trial.

It's probably fair to say that comedy was not Rod Serling's

strong point and this episode is not only unfunny but pretty tedious in the end. Another thing that doesn't help is that this early into The Twilight Zone we are already starting to feel as if we've had one too many of these guardian angel episodes. Orson Bean does his best in the lead role here but soon becomes tiresome - as indeed does the episode as a whole. This is definitely not an episode you'll have anywhere near the top of the pile whenever you do a Twilight Zone marathon. In fact, it's probably one you'll skip altogether. Mr Bevis is a tedious comic relief episode that is probably best avoided. D+

THE AFTER HOURS (Director: Douglas Heyes, Writer: Rod Serling)

"Express elevator to the ninth floor of a department store, carrying Miss Marsha White on a most prosaic, ordinary, run of the mill errand. Miss Marsha White on the ninth floor, specialties department, looking for a gold thimble. The odds are she'll find it, but there are even better odds that she'll find something else, because this isn't just a department store. This happens to be the Twilight Zone."

Marsha White (Anne Francis) is a young women who visits a large and swanky department store to purchase a gold thimble for her mother. However, Marsha's shopping trip turns out to be a surreal and surprising experience indeed...

One of the best Twilight Zone episodes in the history of the show, The After Hours is beautifully, hauntingly (that last act is amazing) directed by Douglas Heyes and has perfect casting with Anne Francis superb as Marsha - our bemused heroine, out shopping for a thimble and discovering a 13th floor in the store that isn't supposed to exist. The twist is great and the compelling atmosphere is wonderfully sustained. There's good support by Elizabeth Allen as a snooty saleslady and John Cornwell is nice casting too as the elevator. You wouldn't think that a department store would be so ripe for a Twilight Zone mystery but it makes a fantastic backdrop for the story here.

This is a darkly magical half an hour of television and simply brilliant at its best. If one had to recommended a handful of Twilight Zone episodes for anyone new to the show to watch first then The After Hours would definitely be a very strong candidate to go on that list. The final revelations are handled very well and the whole episode is masterfully choreographed and rewards the viewer with interest in the final third. It may take until the after hours but Marsha will eventually discover the truth about the store and herself. This is one of the great Twilight Zone episodes and spooky stylish fun all the way. A

THE MIGHTY CASEY (Director: Robert Parrish and Alvin Ganzer, Writer: Rod Serling)

"What you're looking at is a ghost, once alive but now deceased. Once upon a time, it was a baseball stadium that housed a major-league ballclub known as the Hoboken Zephyrs. Now it houses nothing but memories and a wind that stirs in the high grass of what was once an outfield, a wind that sometimes bears a faint, ghostly resemblance to the roar of a crowd that once sat here. We're back in time now, when the Hoboken Zephyrs were still a part of the National League and this mausoleum of memories was an honest-to-Pete stadium. But since this is strictly a story of make-believe, it has to start this way. Once upon a time, in Hoboken, New Jersey, it was tryout day. And though he's not yet on the field, you're about to meet a most unusual fellow, a left-handed pitched named Casey."

A struggling baseball team is given a powerful android pitcher named Casey (Robert Sorrells). When he is banned for not being human, Dr Stillman (Abraham Sofaer) gives Casy a heart and he qualifies again. But now that he has a heart will Casey want to throw his highly dangerous fastballs anymore?

This is a Serling meditation on what it means to be human (Casey loses his unsympathetic competitive edge after receiving the most human of organs) but the theme somewhat lost in this forgettable baseball comic drama. The end result is a dull Twilight Zone - although production troubles apparently dogged this one. This episode was originally shot with Paul Douglas in the Jack Warden role. Douglas though looked ill while shooting it and died of a heart attack a few days after it wrapped. Serling decided (at the expense of his Cayuga Productions rather than CBS) to reshoot the episode with Jack Warden but you wonder why he bothered.

Robert Sorrells is rather awful as the robot and you always struggle to work out how exactly this story even got the green light in the first place. It's like they needed another episode fast so Serling dug up some unfinished and muddled script he found at the bottom of his drawer. The Mighty Casey is one of the more boring episodes in the first season and - alas - joins the likes of Mr Bevis and Execution as something you won't be in a rush to watch again. Even with the modest running time of The Twilight Zone this episode still feels like something of a chore to get through. It's simply dull and forgettable. C

A WORLD OF HIS OWN (Director: Ralph Nelson, Writer: Richard Matheson)

"The home of Mr Gregory West, one of America's most noted playwrights. The office of Mr Gregory West. Mr Gregory West - shy, quiet, and at the moment very happy. Mary - warm, affectionate. And the final ingredient - Mrs Gregory West."

Victoria West (Phyllis Kirk) is surprised when she comes home and finds her husband Gregory (Keenan Wynn) enjoying a drink with a beautiful blonde woman named Mary (Mary La Roche). When she barges into his study though she finds no trace of the mystery woman at all. Gregory explains what has happened. If he describes someone or something into his dictation machine they or it will appear in real life. To make them vanish again all he has to do is throw the tape into the fire. Mary is someone he described into the machine. Victoria doesn't believe him but he demonstrates that it's all true.

A World of His Own is perhaps too lightweight for its own good at times (Rod Serling even makes a comic cameo at the end) but it's likeable enough with the cast decent value and plenty of twists from the pen of Richard Matheson. The story feels very familiar now (Stephen King's Word Processor of the Gods later used a similar conceit) but the dictation machine escapades are an amusing enough way to end what has - with one of two missteps along the way - been a very impressive first year for The Twilight Zone.

As far as comic episodes of Twilight Zone go A World of His Own is one of the less grating ones and although you'd hardly call this a classic it does at least pass the time and supply some entertainment. I'm not sure though that A World of His Own something you would revisit much - if at all. A World of His Own is modest fun but never much more than that. It's a middling end to season one but by no means a complete clunker. B-

The Second Season 1960/61

KING NINE WILL NOT RETURN
(Director: Buzz Kulik, Writer: Rod Serling)

"This is Africa, 1943. War spits out its violence overhead and the sandy graveyard swallows it up. Her name is King Nine, B-25, medium bomber, Twelfth Air Force. On a hot, still morning she took off from Tunisia to bomb the southern tip of Italy. An errant piece of flak tore a hole in a wing tank and, like a wounded bird, this is where she landed, not to return on this day, or any other day."

Captain James Emery (Bob Cummings) wakes up in the North African desert during World War 2 next to the wreckage of his downed B-25 medium bomber. His crew however have mysteriously vanished...

This is a slightly disappointing start to the second year of The Twilight Zone. King Nine Will Not Return has a compelling premise and starts well with the desert intrigue - paranoia soon heightened by the strange mystery that Emery finds himself in. However, the resolution feels like something of a cop-out and the little twist at the end was unnecessary and doesn't make much sense. The premise makes this sound like a terrific episode but it never becomes as good as you want it to be and sort of falls apart in the end. Bob Cummings has to do the heavy lifting in this episode in terms of acting and he's very good but he can't quite mitigate the failure of the script to sustain a satisfying mystery and coda.

King Nine Will Not Return is a decent mystery but one that unravels in the second act - which is a shame because the premise had a lot of potential. King Nine Will Not Return evokes the first ever Twilight Zone episode Where Is Everybody? (central character who finds himself all alone in bizarre circumstances with memory loss) but doesn't reach the same surreal heights. This was based by the way on a true story. The American B-24 Bomber Lady Be Good vanished in 1943 and was later found in 1959 in the Libyan desert by a team of British geologists. The plane's water and ammunition stocks were full but there was not a single trace of the crew anywhere. B-

THE MAN IN THE BOTTLE (Director: Don Medford, Writer: Rod Serling)

"Mr and Mrs Arthur Castle, gentle and infinitely patient people, whose lives have been a hope chest with a rusty lock and a lost set of keys. But in just a moment that hope chest will be opened, and an improbable phantom will try to bedeck the drabness of these two people's failure-laden lives with the gold and precious stones of fulfilment. Mr and Mrs Arthur Castle, standing on the outskirts and about to enter the Twilight Zone."

Arthur Castle (Luthor Adler) and his wife Edna (Vivi Janiss) run an antiques shop and take pity on an old woman trying to sell a worthless bottle. Despite being fairly broke themselves, they give her a dollar for it and the bottle produces a dapper genie (Joseph Ruskin) who tells them they now have four wishes. After wishing for some cracked glass to be mended (just to prove the genie isn't a fake) they ponder what to do with the remaining three wishes. They soon discover though that - naturally - you should be very careful what you wish for in fantasy anthology shows...

The Man In The Bottle is middling episode that riffs on the famous story The Monkey's Paw. This is not bad as far as magical genie episodes go in this anthology shows but always feels a little too pat and predictable to really elevate it too highly in the Twilight Zone pantheon. The main problem is that it feels too derivative as this is the sort of story you feel like you've seen millions of times in these types of shows. The execution is also very lightweight and bland. It's watchable and has its moments but this is definitely not something that lodges in the memory or ever really grabs your attention.

The Man In The Bottle is not terrible but it is decidedly average and continues what has - thus far - been an underwhelming start to season two. This is a pleasant enough episode that unfortunately never really goes anywhere. The best thing here is Joseph Ruskin as the suave but somewhat menacing genie. After watching this episode you could definitely be forgiven for starting to hope that genie in a bottle capers are now given a rest in the show for a while. The Man in the Bottle is probably worth watching but it probably won't figure too highly on any Twilight Zone rewatch piles. B-

NERVOUS MAN IN A FOUR DOLLAR ROOM (Director: Douglas Heyes, Writer: Rod Serling)

"This is Mr Jackie Rhoades, age thirty-four, and where some men leave a mark of their lives as a record of their fragmentary existence on Earth, this man leaves a blot, a dirty, discolored blemish to document a cheap and undistinguished sojourn amongst his betters. What you're about to watch in this room is a strange, mortal combat between a man and himself, for in just a moment Mr Jackie Rhoades, whose life has been given over to fighting adversaries, will find his most formidable opponent in a cheap hotel room that is in reality the outskirts of the Twilight Zone."

Minor league criminal Jackie Roades (Joe Mantill) is ordered to murder someone by his boss and as he agonises over the task in his hotel room room his alter-ego begins to communicate through the mirror. The mirror contains a more ruthless and confident version of Jackie and seems intent on taking control...

Nervous Man In A Four Dollar Room is a fairly strong episode that makes creative use of the constrictive setting to induce paranoia and tension as Jackie struggles to balance the difference sides of his personality - most obviously of course the repressed areas of his id. Douglas Heyes makes excellent use of mirrors and internal monologues and Joe Mantill is well cast as the nervous protagonist.

Nervous Man In A Four Dollar Room would probably stretch your patience somewhat and outstay its welcome if it was an hour long but it works well as a half hour episode and the premise, acting, and direction are all strong enough to hold one's attention and make you interested to see how it turns out in the end. You wouldn't call Nervous Man In A Four Dollar Room a classic but it is a very solid episode that is definitely worth watch. This episode is also one that repays a repeat visit. It's definitely an improvement on the first two episodes of season two. Nervous Man In A Four Dollar Room makes nice use of rear projection and is a decent meditation on the internal struggle between different facets of one's personality. B

A THING ABOUT MACHINES (Director: David Orrick McDearmon, Writer: Rod Serling)

"This is Mr Bartlett Finchley, age forty-eight, a practicing sophisticate who writes very special and very precious things for gourmet magazines and the like. He's a bachelor and a recluse with few friends, only devotees and adherents to the cause of tart sophistry. He has no interests save whatever current annoyances he can put his mind to. He has no purpose to his life except the formulation of day-to-day opportunities to vent his wrath on mechanical contrivances of an age he abhors. In short, Mr Bartlett Finchley is a malcontent, born either too late or too early in the century, and who in just a moment will enter a realm where muscles and the will to fight back are not limited to human beings. Next stop for M. Bartlett Finchley - the Twilight Zone."

Snobbish bachelor Bartlett Finchley (Richard Haydn) has a particular and often violent distaste for the technological bric a brac of the modern world. The machines decide to get revenge...

A Thing About Machines is a silly episode that is easy to dismiss but Richard Haydn enjoyably chews the scenery as Finchley and it's fun when the inanimate objects begin to turn on their unsuspecting owner - with even his car getting in on the act and trying to run him down. What negates A Thing About Machines though is the flat direction and general aimlessness of Serling's script. This episode might actually have worked better had it not been tongue-in-cheek and been played straight as a horror yarn (though to be fair to Serling it would probably be hard to make a straight horror episode featuring a man being attacked by his electrical razor).

This episode passes the time but it's very silly and throwaway and doesn't have much ambition. A Thing About Machines definitely feels like Twilight Zone in third gear and treading water. It's not an episode that anyone will dredge up when talking about the best entries in this classic show. The Twilight Zone would make a similar episode in a later season called You Drive. Out of the two episodes, You Drive is more memorable than A Thing About Machines. B-

THE HOWLING MAN (Director: Douglas Heyes, Writer: Charles Beaumont)

"The prostrate form of Mr David Ellington, scholar, seeker of truth and, regrettably, finder of truth. A man who will shortly arise from his exhaustion to confront a problem that has tormented mankind since the beginning of time. A man who knocked on a door seeking sanctuary and found instead the outer edges of the Twilight Zone."

David Ellington (HM Wynant) is a tourist in Europe who takes shelter in an old castle during a storm. The religious sect who run the castle have what appears to be an ordinary man held hostage. Ellington is appalled by this and protests but is told the hostage is the Devil...

One of the great Twilight Zone episodes, The Howling Man induces a rich sense of atmosphere from the opening scenes and never allows this Gothic aura to relent. Wynant is a good window into the story as Ellington and the episode builds to a compelling last act. This sharp turn towards classic horror for The Twilight Zone reaps rich dividends here.

John Carradine is great here as Brother Jerome - the leader of the sect. Ellington has to decide who he trusts the most. The apparently innocent man being held captive or Brother Jerome.

The drenched, cold, hungry and exhausted Ellington wanders inside looking for shelter but hears a howling noise coming from somewhere. When he investigates he finds a man (Robin Hughes) locked in a cell down below. The man seems perfectly ordinary and harmless though, cultured even, and tells Ellington he is being held prisoner against his will just because he kissed someone in public and that the sect who run the castle are insane.

Are these monks dangerous fanatics who have taken their beliefs too far or could the man really be (gulp) the Devil himself? The captive man is only kept in place by a piece of wood called The Staff of Truth. Why hasn't the captive man simply removed the wood if this is all mystical mumbo jumbo? That's the fun of the story and where the tension comes in. The Howling Man is very Gothic and mysterious and an excellent episode. It's a really compelling little yarn and the vivid sense of atmosphere is fantastic. The Howling Man is terrific stuff and the first classic episode of season three. A-

THE EYE OF THE BEHOLDER (Director: Douglas Heyes, Writer: Rod Serling)

"Suspended in time and space for a moment, your introduction to Miss Janet Tyler, who lives in a very private world of darkness, a universe whose dimensions are the size, thickness, length of a swath of bandages that cover her face. In a moment we'll go back into this room and also in a moment we'll look under those bandages, keeping in mind, of course, that we're not to be surprised by what we see, because this isn't just a hospital, and this patient 307 is not just a woman. This happens to be the Twilight Zone, and Miss Janet Tyler, with you, is about to enter it."

Janet Tyler (Maxine Stuart) lies in a darkened hospital under bandages anxiously waiting to see if her hideously disfigured face has finally been altered enough to stop her being a societal outcast. But what constitutes beauty in this strange future society?

The Eye of the Beholder is justifiably famous for the twist when we get the big reveal and finally see Janet's face for the first time - not to mention the faces of those around her. The build up to the revelation is a little on the slow side but it is expertly directed by Heyes and the haunting music by Bernard Herrmann makes for a perfect backdrop. If the twist takes you by surprise (in that you haven't guessed it and haven't been spoiled) then this is definitely one of the more memorable twists in the history of the show - and that's saying something because Twilight Zone is obviously famed for its twist endings.

This story is very dark (quite literally!) in that it plays out in a darkened hospital with great use of shadows and limited light. This draws us into the episode and makes us wonder what on earth is going on and it also adds an unsettling ambience to the whole piece. The story here is about our perceptions of beauty and the pressure to conform in society or look a certain way. As ever with The Twilight Zone, these themes remain depressingly pertinent even today. This is a superbly atmospheric episode and though a little sedate in terms of pacing it is very absorbing and intriguing. B+

NICK OF TIME (Director: Richard L Bare, Writer: Richard Matheson)

"The hand belongs to Mr Don S Carter, male member of a honeymoon team en route across the Ohio countryside to New York City. In one moment, they will be subjected to a gift most humans never receive in a lifetime. For one penny, they will be able to look into the future. The time is now, the place is a little diner in Ridgeview, Ohio, and what this young couple doesn't realize is that this town happens to lie on the outskirts of the Twilight Zone."

Don Carter (William Shatner) and Pat (Patricia Breslin) are newly married and on their way to New York. They take a rest stop in a small town and go into a diner to get a sandwich and some iced coffee. However, their stay in the diner becomes prolonged when Dan becomes obsessed with a penny fortune telling machine on the counter. Dan begins to believe that this machine really can predict the future...

Nick of Time doesn't sound that exciting from a brief synopsis but it actually turns out to be a fantastic Twilight Zone episode. The little demonic fortune telling machine becomes like a third character in the story as it begins to exert a strange hold on Don - much to the annoyance of his wife. What's great about this episode is that it maintains an element of ambiguity and is more about the power of suggestion and our weakness for being superstitious - as opposed to being overtly fantastical. Nothing is too obvious or overt in this story. This is a superb little episode and very subtle.

The little diner is a great backdrop for the story and William Shatner is very good here in an early role. Shatner is pretty straight here and doesn't ham his part at all. Nick of Time is surprisingly gripping and fascinating in the end and definitely an episode you should make time for in any Twilight Zone marathon. The key question in this story is whether the predicting powers of the machine are real or purely a figment of Don's imagination. This question is the foundation on which a great little yarn is spun. Nick of Time lacks the fireworks and scope of other Twilight Zones but is just as spooky and compelling because it's all about suggestion. Shatner and Breslin are surprisingly convincing as the newlyweds with believable chemistry together. A-

THE LATENESS OF THE HOUR (Director: Jack Smeight, Writer: Rod Serling)

"The residence of Dr William Loren, which is in reality a menagerie for machines. We're about to discover that sometimes the product of man's talent and genius can walk amongst us untouched by the normal ravages of time. These are Dr. Loren's robots, built to functional as well as artistic perfection. But in a moment Dr William Loren, wife and daughter will discover that perfection is relative, that even robots have to be paid for, and very shortly will be shown exactly what is the bill."

Dr Loren (John Hoyt) and his wife (Irene Tedrow) live in a large house with lifelike android servants he has created. Their daughter Jana (Ingar Stevens) is increasingly unhappy though in this house and tells her father that if he doesn't get rid of the androids she will leave. Will he concede to this ultimatum?

This is the first episode in season two that was shot on video tape rather than film. Six episodes in all were shot on videotape in what was obviously a cost cutting experiment. Unavoidably, the three videotape episodes look cheap and strange. They just don't feel right. We miss the beautiful film episodes whenever we get one of these cheap looking videotape episodes. That said, The Lateness Of The Hour is mildly interesting and the cast (especially John Hoyt) are pretty good. The premise is sort of intriguing and there is a creepy atmosphere from the concept alone (it would obviously be pretty weird to live in a spooky house full of realistic robot servants).

A weakness here though is that the twist is not exactly impossible to predict. I felt like I knew fairly on where the story was heading and my suspicions were all confirmed. The Lateness of the Hour is unlikely to pull the rug out from under the viewer and subvert your expectations. All in all this is a middling affair but still quite watchable all the same. Perhaps this episode might be slightly better regarded if it had been shot on film? It's possible. Despite its rather crude appearance on videotape, The Lateness Of The Hour is solid enough - thanks in no small part to the polished performance of John Hoyt and the screenplay by Serling: B-

THE TROUBLE WITH TEMPLETON (Director: Buzz Kulik, Writer: E Jack Neuman)

"Pleased to present for your consideration Mr Booth Templeton, serious and successful star of over thirty Broadway plays, who is not quite all right today. Yesterday and its memories is what he wants, and yesterday is what he'll get. Soon his years and his troubles will descend on him in an avalanche. In order not to be crushed, Mr Booth Templeton will escape from his theater and his world and make his debut on another stage in another world that we call the Twilight Zone."

Booth Templeton (Brian Aherne) is a veteran actor who feels increasingly unhappy in the modern world. He pines for the roaring twenties when he was in his prime. What he pines for most of all is his late wife Laura (Pippa Scott). Templeton leaves the theatre one night after an argument and finds himself transported back to 1927. He tracks down his beloved wife but it seems that things in the old days were not quite so golden as he remembers...

The Trouble with Templeton is a wonderfully moving and stylish episode that has one of the greatest scenes in the history of the show. This is the nightclub sequence where everything freezes and Templeton is led to believe that all is not as he remembers. What makes this story moving and interesting is that Templeton suffers from a malady we are all prone to - which is to be romantic about the past and sometimes feel out of place in the modern world.

Change is inevitable but that doesn't mean it is easy. It could be though that we view the past through rose coloured spectacles because we only remember the good stuff. Maybe it wasn't as great as we remember.

The story here is quite complex because Templeton's take on the past might actually be accurate but in order to protect him he can't be made aware of that. This is a beautifully bittersweet Twilight Zone story with a great last act. The Trouble with Templeton is a beautifully directed and poignant episode with a wonderful performance by Aherne as the troubled actor.

Look out for a young Sydney Pollack by the way as the brash theatre director who rubs Templeton up the wrong way.

Thank heavens by the way that The Trouble with Templeton wasn't one of those cheap looking videotape episodes. That would have been an absolute crime! B+

A MOST UNUSUAL CAMERA (Director: John Rich, Writer: Rod Serling)

"A hotel suite that in this instance serves as a den of crime, the aftermath of a rather minor event to be noted on a police blotter, an insurance claim, perhaps a three-inch box on page twelve of the evening paper. Small addenda to be added to the list of the loot: a camera, a most unimposing addition to the flotsam and jetsam that it came with, hardly worth mentioning really, because cameras are cameras, some expensive, some purchasable at five-and-dime stores. But this camera, this one's unusual, because in just a moment we'll watch it inject itself into the destinies of three people. It happens to be a fact that the pictures that it takes can only be developed in the Twilight Zone."

Chester Diedrich (Fred Clark) and wife Paula (Jean Carson) steal a cmera and soon deduce that said camera has magical properties. The camera takes photographs which predict what will happen five minutes into the future. Paula's jailbird brother Woodward (Adam Williams) arrives on the scene and suggests they use the camera to get rich by predicting the winners at the horse racing track. However, with a dwindling amount of photographs left at their disposal these thieves are soon squabbling and inevitably about to experience the Twilight Zone at the sharp end...

The premise of A Most Unusual Camera is hardly original (the story feels like a riff on The Monkey's Paw and is also quite similar to a previous Twilight Zone story called What You Need) but it's at least interesting enough to at least hold your attention. One problem this episode has is that it's all played in a jocular and over the top fashion when it probably would have worked much better as a straight mystery. The performances are over the top and you feel like the cast are trying too hard. The cast here definitely seem to believe they are in a comedy but comedy was not, as we've noted before, Rod Serling's greatest strength.

This is a heavily flawed episode for all of this reasons but I can't find in myself to be too harsh about A Most Unusual Camera because at least it wasn't boring - mostly thanks to the fantasy concept which drives the story. One is modestly engaged and interested throughout the episode and this does mitigate some (if not all) of the flaws in the acting and execution of A Most Unusual Camera. This is fun as far as it goes but not an episode you'd find yourself returning to in a hurry. There are many other episodes that are much more worthy of your time. B-

NIGHT OF THE MEEK (Director: Jack Smight, Writer: Rod Serling)

"This is Mr Henry Corwin, normally unemployed, who once a year takes the lead role in the uniquely popular American institute, that of department-store Santa Claus in a road company version of 'The Night Before Christmas.' But in just a moment Mr Henry Corwin, ersatz Santa Claus, will enter a strange kind of North Pole which is one part the wondrous spirit of Christmas and one part the magic that can only be found in the Twilight Zone."

A drunken department store Santa named Henry Corwin (Art Carney) is fired from his job for always being sozzled. He drowns his sorrows in the nearest bar (still wearing his tatty Santa suit) and then finds a strange bag that can magically dispense any gift he wants. Now invested with the real powers of Santa, Corwin decides to spread as much joy and generosity as he can with this magical find...

Night of the Meek was one of Rod Serling's favourite Twilight Zones and he apparently used to screen it at Christmas for his friends and family. It's certainly a nice episode and a pleasant experience but it does become a trifle cloying and sentimental at times. Still, I suppose you'd have to be a real life Scrooge to

complain abut this one too much. It's just a nice charming
Christmas yarn where a man gets a chance to bring some
magical Christmas spirit into the lives of 'hopeless and
dreamless'.

It's a shame really that Night of the Meek is one of the dreaded
videotape episodes because the seasonal sets are very nice and
cosy and definitely would have been even better if shot on film.
Night of the Meek is probably a little overrated in the Twilight
Zone canon but it is generally an enjoyable experience and Art
Carney is very good as our unexpected Christmas hero. This is
somewhat saccharine and obvious but you'd have to have a
heart of stone not to enjoy Night of the Meek. One to watch on
Christmas Eve. B

DUST (Director: Douglas Heyes, Writer: Rod Serling)

"There was a village, built of crumbling clay and rotting wood,
and it squatted ugly under a broiling sun like a sick and mangy
animal wanting to die. This village had a virus, shared by its
people. It was the germ of squalor, of hopelessness, of a loss of
faith. For the faithless, the hopeless, the misery-laden, there is
time, ample time, to engage in one of the other pursuits of
men. They begin to destroy themselves."

A carnival huckster and charlatan named Sykes (Thomas
Gomez) decides to make some money at a public execution in
the Old West by pretending that he has some magic dust which
can save a man about to be hung. In reality, it's just a bag of
dirt. Or is it?

Dust is one of the more forgettable Twilight Zone episodes and
seems to take an age to get to what is a fairly underwhelming
conclusion. The depiction of time and place is good and the
actors are passable but the story is dreadfully dull and the
story is simply never that interesting at all. You expect Sykes to

get some sort of cosmic karma Twilight Zone comeuppance but this never happens in the end. One presumes the point of the story is that people are capable of being redeemed and seeing the error of their ways but even so this episode limps to a pretty tame resolution.

Dust is arguably the dullest episode of Twilight Zone thus far in the show and not something you'll be in a rush to sit through again. As far as the Old West episodes of The Twilight Zone go this is definitely one of the weakest. The intention of the story here was to depict a town so drenched in apathy and laziness that they can't even rouse any enthusiasm to question the local justice system. While that might be an interesting idea on paper it - unfortunately - leads to a tediously languid and slow episode which, even with the modest running time, becomes something of a slog to get through in the end. Dust is well made but simply boring. C-

BACK THERE (Director: David Orrick McDearmon, Writer: Rod Serling)

"Witness a theoretical argument, Washington D.C., the present. Four intelligent men talking about an improbable thing like going back in time. A friendly debate revolving around a simple issue: could a human being change what has happened before? Interesting and theoretical because who ever heard of a man going back in time, before tonight, that is. Because this is the Twilight Zone."

Peter Corrigan (Russell Johnson) discusses the theoretical paradoxes of time travel in his gentleman's club and when he leaves he finds himself transported to 1865. Corrigan decides to foil Lincoln's assassination but he discovers that altering the course of time and history is a lot more complex than one might think...

The premise of Back There sounds like a lot of fun (in fact, it's quite similar to the enjoyable Stephen King book 11/22/63) but for some reason it never quite translates into a classic Twilight Zone episode. Back There is rife with plotholes and also commits the unpardonable sin of being rather dull at times. It's a shame really because this had the potential to be a fun little episode but it never takes off and grabs the viewer in the way it should.

The cast are serviceable enough and Corrigan's obstacles in his quest to save Lincoln do at least keep you mildly engaged but you can't help feeling that a time travel story of this nature should have been a lot more memorable and a lot more watchable than Back There ever turns out to be. You wouldn't say this was an out and out clunker but it is depressingly average and never really does justice to the interesting premise. The Twilight Zone would use that familiar fantasy staple of the time travel yarn many times and this is disappointingly one of the more forgettable examples.

Back There feels rather like a pale rehash of Serling's The Time Element in its general story. The Time Element was much more entertaining and intriguing than Back There ultimately manages to be. If you like time travel stories you might enjoy this more than I did but I wouldn't go in with your expectations too high. Despite the interesting premise, Back There doesn't score highly on the logic front and never really takes off. This is an episode that sounds a lot more interesting than it actually plays. C+

THE WHOLE TRUTH (Director: James Sheldon, Writer: Rod Serling)

"This, as the banner already has proclaimed, is Mr Harvey Hunnicut, an expert on commerce and con jobs, a brash, bright, and larceny-loaded wheeler and dealer who, when the good lord passed out a conscience, must have gone for a beer and missed out. And these are a couple of other characters in our story: a little old man and a Model A car - but not just any old man and not just any Model A. There's something very special about the both of them. As a matter of fact, in just a few moments they'll give Harvey Hunnicut something that he's never experienced before. Through the good offices of a little magic, they will unload on Mr Hunnicut the absolute necessity to tell the truth. Exactly where they come from is conjectural, but as to where they're heading for, this we know, because all of them - and you - are on the threshold of the Twilight Zone."

A shifty and dubious car salesman named Harvey Hunnicut (Jack Carson) ends up with a magical car which - for the first time in his life - makes him tell the truth. As you might imagine, this is not a great development for Harvey's profit margins...

The Whole Truth is another of those cheap looking videotape episodes and pretty insufferable. This plays like a failed pilot for some 1950s dire sitcom and is one of those Twilight Zone episodes that is a chore to sit through. It is not only unfunny but absolutely tedious to boot. The script somehow manages to end up touching upon politics and the Cold War but by this point you've probably lost interest anyway. This is a rather baffling episode on the whole and one of those Twilight Zones where you wonder how it even got the green light in the first place. I suppose with so many episodes to produce they couldn't strike gold every week and a few clunkers were unavoidable.

The Whole Truth is a perfect illustration of why the videotape experiment doesn't work. Videotape makes the show look like some bargain basement stagebound live drama. That rich Twilight Zone residue and atmosphere is lost when they don't shoot on film. The "object as truth serum" plot device occurred more than once in The Twilight Zone but this is by far the worst example. The Whole Truth is one for Twilight Zone completists only. This definitely wouldn't entice anyone new to the show to watch more episodes. In fact, it would probably have the opposite effect. D-

THE INVADERS (Director: Douglas Heyes, Writer: Richard Matheson)

"This is one of the out-of-the-way places, the unvisited places, bleak, wasted, dying. This is a farmhouse, handmade, crude, a house without electricity or gas, a house untouched by progress. This is the woman who lives in the house, a woman who's been alone for many years, a strong, simple woman whose only problem up until this moment has been that of acquiring enough food to eat, a woman about to face terror which is even now coming at her from the Twilight Zone."

A mute woman (Agnes Moorhead) in a primitive and isolated farmhouse has a frightening encounter with tiny alien invaders...

After three disappointing episodes on the spin, season two two thankfully finds its mojo again with The Invaders - a simple but enjoyably atmospheric and strange thriller which turns out to be a lot of fun and has a nice twist at the end. Agnes Moorhead has no dialogue in this episode but gives a convincing performance as a terrified woman who has to battle these miniature spacemen who have unexpectedly turned up at her house for reasons she can't fathom.

This episode becomes very gripping and the battle between the woman and the invaders is a lot of fun. The alien invaders are basically depicted by use of what look like wind up toys and puppets. This is definitely on the hokey side (especially from a modern point of view where state of the art computer effects are commonplace in everything) and they do look ridiculous at times but the premise is so good you simply go along with it and get into the story. Besides, hokey special effects in old sci-fi are not without charm today in our headache inducing CGI festooned age. You have to love the little crackle sound of the alien ray guns in The Invaders!

The little metallic spacemen are rather creepy with the tiny thud of their footsteps and the crackle of their ray guns. Director Douglas Heyes makes good use of the farmhouse and shadowy light as this enjoyably bonkers but gripping story plays out. The Invaders is a lot of fun and the simplicity of the premise turns out to be its strength. A-

A PENNY FOR YOUR THOUGHTS (Director: James Sheldon, Writer: George Clayton Johnson)

"Mr. Hector B Poole, resident of the Twilight Zone. Flip a coin and keep flipping it. What are the odds? Half the time it will come up heads, half the time tails. But in one freakish chance in a million, it'll land on its edge. Mr. Hector B Poole, a bright human coin, on his way to the bank."

Mild mannered and put upon office worker Hector Poole (Dick York) is given the power to read minds. Will he like what he hears?

A Penny For Your Thoughts is a fairly throwaway lighter episode but it's reasonably entertaining for what it is and one of the less grating comic episodes of The Twilight Zone. There's quite an interesting theme to this episode in that we see how one's thoughts are not necessarily in sync with one's actions. Hector discovers that being able to read minds might be more trouble than it is worth. It also gives him a rather jaundiced view on humanity because he discovers that those around him are secretly up to all sorts of schemes. Poole's attempts to use this power to do good backfire on him in modestly comical fashion so he begins to wonder if he shouldn't be more self serving - especially where his grumpy boss Mr Bagby (Dan Tobin) is concerned.

Dick York (best known for Bewitched) is a likeable enough window through which the story is told and while this episode is probably not one that will stick in the memory for very long it does at least pass the time. The script is actually quite dense and clever in that an awful lot of incident and plot is crammed into the story without becoming confusing or jarringly clunky. A Penny For Your Thoughts is no great shakes but it is an agreeable enough time waster and likeable enough. A Penny For Your Thoughts is a lighter episode but a clever one. The humour seems less forced here because it is deftly written by George Clayton Johnson. B-

TWENTY-TWO (Director: Jack Smight, Writer: Rod Serling)

"This is Miss Liz Powell. She's a professional dancer and she's in the hospital as a result of overwork and nervous fatigue. And at this moment we have just finished walking with her in a nightmare. In a moment she'll wake up and we'll remain at her side. The problem here is that both Miss Powell and you will reach a point where it might be difficult to decide which is reality and which is nightmare, a problem uncommon perhaps but rather peculiar to the Twilight Zone."

Liz Powell (Barbara Nichols) is a dancer suffering from exhaustion who is confined to a hospital ward. Each night she is plagued by nightmares about Room 22 - which just happens to be the morgue. In her nightmares Liz is shepherded to this room as if it is her unavoidable fate. She begins to suspect the visions are real but her doctor insists she is simply having bad dreams...

This is based on The Bus-Conductor by EF Benson - which inspired a segment in the classic 1945 Ealing compendium horror film Dead of Night. Twenty-Two is a decent enough supernatural mystery that is competently made but suffers slightly from the fact we've seen this type of story in a gazillion horror anthology shows and films. The sense of dread and foreboding here is good though and in terms of atmosphere this ranks as one of the bleaker Twilight Zones - all to the strength of the story.

The twist at the end is quite good too and serves as an appropriately chilling coda to this spine tingling mystery. By the way, look out for Lost in Space star Jonathan Harris. Harris is always fun in anything he turns up in. Twenty-Two never quite elevates itself into a classic Twilight Zone episode and that's probably a result of the subject matter here feeling a little on the derivative side but it is fairly engrossing and it's nice to see a more overtly horror centred episode of the show. Twenty-Two is a fair enough chiller about premonition and fate. The performances are a tad ripe but it's not bad. B-

THE ODYSSEY OF FLIGHT 33 (Director: Justus Addiss, Writer: Rod Serling)

"You're riding on a jet airliner en route from London to New York. You're at 35,000 feet atop an overcast and roughly fifty-five minutes from Idlewild Airport. But what you've seen occur inside the cockpit of this plane is no reflection on the aircraft or the crew. It's a safe, well-engineered, perfectly designed machine, and the men you've just met are a trained, cool, highly efficient team.

The problem is simply that the plane is going too fast and there is nothing within the realm of knowledge or at least logic to explain it. Unbeknownst to passenger and crew, this airplane is heading into an uncharted region well off the beaten track of commercial travellers. It's moving into the Twilight Zone. What you're about to see we call The Odyssey of Flight 33."

Trans-Ocean Airways Flight 33 is on its way from New York to London. After being buffeted by incredible and inexplicable winds the plane is thrown back in time. How are you supposed to land a plane if there are dinosaurs below?!

If you've ever wondered what would happen if the aeroplane you were on was inexplicably catapulted back through time to an age of flying Pterodactyls then The Odyssey of Flight 33 will provide some of the answers you've probably never been looking for. The Odyssey of Flight 33 is justifiably regarded to be a classic episode of The Twilight Zone and is good (if somewhat silly) fun with a fantastic mystery and the solid presence of John Anderson as the pilot. It's a nice idea to have a Twilight Zone set on a plane (an idea they would of course return to in famous fashion later on in the show) and this is classic Twilight Zone in the way that the characters are thrust into a baffling and seemingly impossible mystery and must desperately try to make sense of it before it is all too late.

It helps that even with a story this outlandish the cast all play it totally straight and so give the drama (as fantastical as it might be) more weight and authenticity. Look out for the enjoyably old school stop motion dinosaur in this episode. Here, the drama comes from the crew desperately running out of time and throwing their last reserves of fuel into a desperate attempt to pick up enough speed to get back to their own time. Rod Serling actually consulted his aviation engineer brother when he was writing this and therefore the technical dialogue between the crew sounds credibly authentic.

The Twilight Zone returned to the time travel well many times but this is probably the most accomplished example. The dinosaur footage in this was actually lifted from the 1960 bargain basement science fiction film Dinosaurus! The Brontosaurus model was used here.

The Odyssey of Flight 33 is very enjoyable on the whole and definitely one of the most memorable episodes of The Twilight Zone. The wonderful premise alone is hard to forget! It's a daft mystery but played wonderfully straight - the story always intriguing and gripping. Gratuitous trivia - the Tyrannosaurus from Dinosaurus! was used in Gilligan's Island. A-

MR DINGLE, THE STRONG (Director: John Brahn, Writer: Rod Serling)

"Uniquely American institution known as the neighborhood bar. Reading left to right are Mr Anthony O'Toole, proprietor who waters his drinks like geraniums but who stands foursquare for peace and quiet and for booths for ladies. This is Mr Joseph J Callahan, an unregistered bookie, whose entire life is any sporting event with two sides and a set of odds. His idea of a meeting at the summit is any dialogue between a catcher and a pitcher with more than one man on base. And this animated citizen is every anonymous bettor who ever dropped rent money on a horse race, a prize fight, or a floating crap game, and who took out his frustrations and his insolvency on any vulnerable fellow barstool companion within arm's and fist's reach.

And this is Mr Luther Dingle, a vacuum-cleaner salesman whose volume of business is roughly that of a valet at a hobo convention. He's a consummate failure in almost everything but is a good listener and has a prominent jaw. And these two unseen gentlemen are visitors from outer space. They are about to alter the destiny of Luther Dingle by leaving him a legacy, the kind you can't hardly find no more. In just a moment, a sad-faced perennial punching bag who missed even the caboose of life's gravy train will take a short constitutional into that most unpredictable region that we refer to as the Twilight Zone."

As an experiment, Martian scientists gives a vacuum struggling cleaner salesman named Luthor Dingle (Burgess Meredith) the strength of three hundred men. Mr Dingle soon becomes something of a celebrity...

Mr. Dingle, the Strong is the black sheep of the usually excellent Burgess Meredith Twilight Zones and a pretty pointless half hour of television. This is a comic episode but not terribly funny in the least (I'd probably be repeating myself by now if I said that comic episodes were not the usually brilliant Rod Serling's greatest gift as a writer but it's probably worth repeating one more time in the case of this episode). There's not much of a twist here and the antics with Luthor showing off his powers of super strength soon become rather tiresome. He lifts statues, tears telephone books and becomes a minor celebrity.

Burgess Meredith is committed and enthusiastic as ever but even he can't do much with this silly and somewhat dull story. It's a shame really because there's quite a good cast in this one with familiar faces like James Millhollin and Don Rickles popping up. Mr. Dingle, the Strong is saddled with some very hokey alien designs (in mitigation they are deliberately whimsical and silly but - even so - still terrible) and a rather underwhelming punchline.

Surprisingly though the consensus on this episode doesn't seem to be as universally negative as my reaction. Some fans do seem to genuinely find this episode amusing - and that's fine because we all obviously have different tastes. If you like the more comic episodes and love Burgess Meredith (and who doesn't?) then it is possible you might get more out of this than I did. Sadly, I personally find Mr. Dingle, the Strong to be completely forgettable and quite dull in the end. D+

STATIC (Director: Buzz Kulik, Writer: Charles Beaumont)

"No one ever saw one quite like that, because that's a very special sort of radio. In its day, circa 1935, its type was one of the most elegant consoles on the market. Now, with its fabric-covered speakers, its peculiar yellow dial, its serrated knobs, it looks quaint and a little strange. Mr. Ed Lindsay is going to find out how strange very soon when he tunes in to the Twilight Zone."

Ed Lindsay (Dean Jagger) is a cranky old man who shares a boarding house with other senior citizens. Ed finds an old radio in the basement which seems to tune into shows from a bygone era. This magical radio rekindles memories of his younger years and the days when he was engaged to Vinnie Broun (Carmen Matthews) - who also lives in the boarding house. Is it too late for Ed to have a second chance at happiness?

Static is another of the videotape episodes but for some reason this is less of a problem here than the others shot on video. Maybe it's because the setting is simple and the story is likeable enough. This show did several stories about old folks who take an excursion in the Twilight Zone and most of them were agreeable enough. Static is no exception and is a bittersweet little yarn that passes the time and is quite moving at its best.

One interesting thing about this episode is that it's a sort of tribute to the golden age of radio. By the early sixties television had overtaken radio as the main medium of entertainment and so - already - radio was starting to be slightly seen as a bygone sort of thing. Static is another Twilight Zone episode which mines a theme that is recurring in the show - the desire to turn back the clock and escape from the circumstances of one's present situation. Static is no classic but it's fine for what it is and one of the better of the several episodes shot on videotape. B-

THE PRIME MOVER (Director: Richard L Bare, Writer: Charles Beaumont)

"Portrait of a man who thinks and thereby gets things done. Mr. Jimbo Cobb might be called a prime mover, a talent which has to be seen to be believed. In just a moment, he'll show his friends and you how he keeps both feet on the ground and his head in the Twilight Zone."

Ace Larsen (Dane Clark) and Jimbo (Buddy Ebsen) are friends who work in a cafe. Ace realises that Jimbo has psychokinetic abilities and insists they head to Las Vegas to clean up at the casinos. Jimbo is not terribly comfortable with this plan though and begins to tire of using his powers simply for the pursuit of money...

The Prime Mover is another of those middling middle ranking sort of Twilight Zones episodes. It's fairly entertaining but one wouldn't place it near the Twilight Zone top table.

The contrast between the two lead actors is good though and gives this most of its juice. Ace is confident and brash while Jimbo is more laid-back and shy. There's an obvious message here about how money and the pursuit of money is not the be all and end all of life. It's really the arc of Ace that drives this story. He must come to realise that the simple things (like love and friendship) are what make life worth living - not wealth and greed.

It's quite good fun to have another casino story in The Twilight Zone and The Prime Mover passes the time well enough. The ending is reasonably satisfying and this is generally a pleasant experience if not something that will stay lodged in the memory very long in the way that the top tier Twilight Zone episodes tend to do. The Prime Mover is decent enough but never much more than that. It's certainly an episode that is worth watching though. B-

LONG DISTANCE CALL (Director: James Sheldon, Writer: Charles Beaumont)

"As must be obvious, this is a house hovered over by Mr Death, that omnipresent player to the third and final act of every life. And it's been said, and probably rightfully so, that what follows this life is one of the unfathomable mysteries, an area of darkness which we the living reserve for the dead - or so it is said. For in a moment, a child will try to cross that bridge which separates light and shadow, and of course he must take the only known route, that indistinct highway through the region we call the Twilight Zone."

Five year-old Billy (Billy Mumy) is very close to his grandmother Grandma Bayles (Lili Darvas). Grandma Bayles gives Billy a toy plastic telephone on his birthday but when she dies Billy claims he can still speak to his grandmother on the toy phone...

Long Distance Call is probably the best of Twilight Zone's videotape episodes and a pretty dark sort of story. It's very creepy when Billy claims he is talking to his deceased grandmother on the toy phone and things get even darker when Billy begins to try and injure himself - as if someone wants him to join them in the great beyond. The story has a nice supernatural element and is essentially about grandma learning to let go of Billy so he can get on with his life. While dark it does have an uplifting sort of quality by the time of its conclusion.

Child actor Billy Mumy is decent enough here as the troubled boy and this, as we shall see, would not be his last contribution to The Twilight Zone. His next episode would one of the most memorable in the history of the show. It's a slight shame that Long Distance Call wasn't shot on film because these videotape episodes always seem slightly weird and 'off' visually but - generally - this is a pretty solid episode and good for what it is.

This is a pretty dark episode but works as a ghost story and has a satisfying resolution. It was apparently subject to a last minute rewrite by Serling (who visited the set and didn't like the dialogue at the end). These changes appear to have been successful. B

A HUNDRED YARDS OVER THE RIM (Director: Buzz Kulick, Writer: Rod Serling)

"The year is 1847, the place is the territory of New Mexico, the people are a tiny handful of men and women with a dream. Eleven months ago, they started out from Ohio and headed west. Someone told them about a place called California, about a warm sun and a blue sky, about rich land and fresh air, and at this moment almost a year later they've seen nothing but cold, heat, exhaustion, hunger, and sickness. This man's name is Christian Horn. He has a dying eight year-old son and a heartsick wife, and he's the only one remaining who has even a fragment of the dream left. Mr Chris Horn, who's going over the top of a rim to look for water and sustenance and in a moment will move into the Twilight Zone."

Christian Horn (Cliff Robertson) is part of a wagon train on the way to California in 1847. There's a problem though because his son has fallen ill and in desperate need of medicine and water. Horn breaks off from the group to look for a town and clambers over a rim. The sight that greets him is perplexing and astonishing. Modern telegraph poles, a highway with trucks, and a 1961 diner. It appears that Horn has emerged one hundred years into the future...

A Hundred Yards Over the Rim is a wonderful Twilight Zone episode which perfectly illustrates how the simplest stories can often be the best ones. Cliff Robertson, in his first trip to the Twilight Zone, is excellent and authentic as Horn and the sense of time and place is very believable in the intro to this story. Things of course take a fantastical turn when Horn is somehow catapulted into the future but all the same this is a rewarding low-key sort of Twilight Zone episode rather than one where all sorts of crazy things happen.

The story here is clever and perfectly satisfying in the way it resolves itself and A Hundred Yards Over the Rim is a very deft blend of drama and fantasy that works all the better for being played perfectly straight. Look out for John Astin in this episode too and John Crawford and Evans Evans (no typo - that's her name!) offer nice support as the diner owners the perplexed Horn encounters. A Hundred Yards Over the Rim is an excellent Twilight Zone entry and a very satisfying little drama. Although not an awful lot happens in the story it wraps up in a clever and satisfying way and is an interesting and absorbing fish out of water tale with a big dose of fantasy and science fiction. Wonderful performance by Robertson as the perplexed Horn. A-

THE RIP VAN WINKLE CAPER (Director: Justus Addiss, Writer: Rod Serling)

"Introducing four experts in the questionable art of crime. Mr Farwell, expert on noxious gases, former professor with a doctorate in both chemistry and physics. Mr Erbie, expert on mechanical engineering. Mr Brooks, expect in the use of firearms and other weaponry. And Mr DeCruz, expert in demolition and various forms of destruction. The time is now and the place is a mountain cave in Death Valley, USA. In just a moment, these four men will utilize the services of a truck placed in cosmoline, loaded with a hot heist cooled off by a century of sleep, and then take a drive into the Twilight Zone."

A gang of thieves led by Professor Farwell (Oscar Beregi, Jr) steal $1 million in gold bullion. Farwell, who fancies himself as a criminal genius, has come up with he thinks is a brilliant plan. They will go into suspended animation in stasis pods (located in an old cave so they aren't disturbed) for one hundred years and then awaken one hundred years in the future. Farwell figures that one hundred years from now their crime will be forgotten and they will be presumed dead so no one will be looking for them anymore. And that gold is sure to be worth even more in the future isn't it? What can possibly go wrong with this masterful plan? Well, this being the Twilight Zone, quite a lot as it turns out...

They say there is no honour among thieves and that's definitely the case with the characters in The Rip Van Winkle Caper. Once they awaken they soon begin to bicker and turn on one another and it ends up as a bad tempered battle of wits between Farwell and DeCruz (Simon Oakland) as they haul their gold across a long desert road. The Rip Van Winkle Caper is a lot of fun and a very enjoyable half hour of television. It's fun right from the start when the characters must enter the stasis pods in the cave (wonder if this what gave Serling the idea for the stasis pods at the start of The Planet of the Apes?). So what you essentially get here is an entertaining crime caper with some sci-fi trappings.

Oscar Beregi, Jr is entertainingly pompous as Farwell - a man who, as we shall find out - is not quite as clever as he had assumed. Beregi plays Farwell like a low-level Bond villain and his presence elevates this crime caper and makes it even more enjoyable. Simon Oakland is good too although his role is slightly more constrictive in that's basically there to provide friction and give Farwell a hard time. The Rip Van Winkle Caper is a very enjoyable episode and has a very satisfying and classically Twilight Zone-ish twist at the end. The twist here is deliciously ironic. B+

THE SILENCE (Director: Boris Sagal, Writer: Rod Serling)

"The note that this man is carrying across a club room is in the form of a proposed wager, but it's the kind of wager that comes without precedent. It stands alone in the annals of bet-making as the strangest game of chance ever offered by one man to another. In just a moment, we'll see the terms of the wager and what young Mr. Tennyson does about it. And in the process, we'll witness all parties spin a wheel of chance in a very bizarre casino called the Twilight Zone."

At a swanky gentleman's club, snobby Colonel Archie Taylor (Franchot Tone) is increasingly annoyed by the chatty and popular young Jamie Tennyson (Liam Sullivan). Taylor proposes a wager to Tennyson. He will give him one million dollars on one condition. Tennyson simply has to stay silent and not speak for one year...

The Silence has a great premise and although it strains credibility (would anyone really agree to give up a year of their life in this way?) it does make for a gripping and absorbing episode. Tennyson has financial trouble - which I suppose explains why he agrees to the wager - and is also eager to take Taylor to the cleaners. Tennyson is then placed in a room where he can be recorded and monitored for one year just to make he adheres to the stipulation that he not speak.

One of the most enjoyable aspects to the story here is the way that the urbane Taylor becomes increasingly rattled and concerned when Tennyson lasts much longer in this strange wager than he had expected. The battle of will between the two main characters is what drives the story and makes it interesting. Will Tennyson claim that million dollars? Well, you'll just have to find out for yourself.

The Silence is a very interesting episode in that it has no magical or fantastical elements but still feels like it has a lot Twilight Zone DNA and residue. This is definitely a very watchable and above average episode. There's a very good twist at the end too. You probably wouldn't quite put The Silence at the Twilight Zone top table but it is a very good little episode though. It's a good episode with a macabre twist in the tale. Superb performances from Franchot Tone and Liam Sullivan.

The central idea behind The Silence is a clever and intriguing one. Could you stay silent for a whole year if a million dollars was at stake? B+

SHADOW PLAY (Director: John Brahm, Writer: Charles Beaumont)

"Adam Grant, a nondescript kind of man found guilty of murder and sentenced to the electric chair. Like every other criminal caught in the wheels of justice he's scared, right down to the marrow of his bones. But it isn't prison that scares him, the long, silent nights of waiting, the slow walk to the little room, or even death itself. It's something else that holds Adam Grant in the hot, sweaty grip of fear, something worse than any punishment this world has to offer, something found only in the Twilight Zone."

Adam Grant (Dennis Weaver) is on Death Row in prison and nearing his execution. However, he feels as if he has been in this situation many times before as if trapped in some repeating time loop. Is this real or simply a vivid nightmare?

Shadow Play is a solid episode powered by a committed performance by Dennis Weaver as the incarcerated man apparently trapped in a terrible nightmare. The dreamlike atmosphere of the story is put across on the screen and there are many surreal flourishes that pay off the observant viewer - like the supporting cast frequently switching characters as if they are all in a nightmarish play being performed in Grant's imagination. Shadow Play is wonderfully paranoid and sustained.

This is quite a clever Twilight Zone and those paying attention closely will get some rewarding pay-offs as the story progresses. This is sort of Kafka meets Groundhog Day meets The Twilight Zone and it all rattles along at a good pace and holds one's attention throughout. The supporting cast are fine and Shadow Play builds to a fairly satisfying third act. This episode (happily) continues what has been a strong batch of final stories for season two of The Twilight Zone. This is a suspenseful, complex and gripping episode that explores the shadow realm of the nightmare. Imagine if you had a nightmare you couldn't escape from that seemed to be stuck on a constant loop. It's a good episode about the nature of reality. B+

THE MIND AND THE MATTER (Director: John Brahm, Writer: Charles Beaumont)

"A brief if frenetic introduction to Mr Archibald Beechcroft, a child of the twentieth century, a product of the population explosion, and one of the inheritors of the legacy of progress. Mr Beechcroft again. This time act two of his daily battle for survival. And in just a moment, our hero will begin his personal one-man rebellion against the mechanics of his age, and to do so he will enlist certain aids available only in the Twilight Zone."

Office worker Archibald Beechcroft (Shelly Berman) is fed-up with fighting his way to work through crowds of people and equally annoyed by his co-workers in his overcrowded place of employment. After acquiring a book about mental powers, Beechcroft discovers he can make something happen merely by thinking about it. Why not make other people disappear? The world be nicer and quieter without other people wouldn't it?

The Mind And The Matter has quite an interesting premise (most of us have had a fantasy about having the world to ourself for a day!) but the arc of Beechcroft is rather predictable in that we just know he'll end up learning that people make the world what it is and you'd rather have them around than not. The main problem with this episode is that it's one of those jaunty comical episodes so everything in the story has less weight or consequence than it would have done with a straight drama or mystery.

The Mind And The Matter is never terribly funny either

although it is quite inventive when Beechcroft encounters multiple versions of himself. The world created here where everyone looks like Shelly Berman seems to rather anticipate the film Being John Malkovich! You wouldn't say that The Mind And The Matter is boring but it is fairly forgettable and feels like the show treading water - especially in comparison to the strong and ambitious episodes that preceded it in the previous weeks. Shelly Berman, by the way, was much later Larry David's dad in Curb Your Enthusiasm. He's ok in this but it's hardly a classic episode of the show. C+

WILL THE REAL MARTIAN PLEASE STAND UP? (Director: Montgomery Pittman, Writer: Rod Serling)

"Wintry February night, the present. Order of events: a phone call from a frightened woman notating the arrival of an unidentified flying object, then the check-out you've just witnessed with two state troopers verifying the event, but with nothing more enlightening to add beyond evidence of some tracks leading across the highway to a diner. You've heard of trying to find a needle in a haystack? Well, stay with us now and you'll be part of an investigating team whose mission is not to find that proverbial needle. No, their task is even harder. They've got to find a Martian in a diner, and in just a moment you'll search with them, because you've just landed in the Twilight Zone."

A small group of bus passengers take refuge in a diner during a snow blizzard. However, there is evidence that a UFO crashed nearby and footprints from the site lead straight to the diner. Two police officers must go to the diner and see if they can deduce which person is the imposter...

Will The Real Martian Please Stand Up? is a brilliant Twilight Zone episode with oodles of atmosphere and a fantastic premise. The brilliant thing about this episode is that it is broadly what you could describe as a comic episode and yet the mystery is not diluted in the least by the humour. There is a perfect blend between levity and mystery here that makes it Serling's best ever comic script. Much of the credit for this must go to Jack Elam as an eccentric man in the diner who seems to find the entire situation amusing. Elam is very funny in Will The Real Martian Please Stand Up?

The viewer has to play detective in this episode and try and deduce who the alien imposter might be. The answer to that question supplies a terrific double twist at the end. The cast here is great - especially John Hoyt as the suspicious businessman Hoyt. What's really great about Will The Real Martian Please Stand Up? is that it has a perfect setting for a Twilight Zone story in that these characters are trapped in a constrictive location where strange things are abounding. The diner jukebox keeps coming on and off and the lights suddenly seem to have a life of their own. Will The Real Martian Please Stand Up? is definitely one of the great Twilight Zone episodes and tremendous fun from start to finish. A

THE OBSOLETE MAN (Director: Elliot Silverstein, Writer: Rod Serling)

"You walk into this room at your own risk, because it leads to the future, not a future that will be but one that might be. This is not a new world, it is simply an extension of what began in the old one. It has patterned itself after every dictator who has ever planted the ripping imprint of a boot on the pages of history since the beginning of time. It has refinements, technological advances, and a more sophisticated approach to the destruction of human freedom. But like every one of the superstates that preceded it, it has one iron rule: logic is an enemy and truth is a menace. This is Mr Romney Wordsworth, in his last forty-eight hours on Earth. He's a citizen of the State but will soon have to be eliminated, because he is built out of flesh and because he has a mind. Mr Romney Wordsworth, who will draw his last breaths in the Twilight Zone."

In a future totalitarian state, librarian Romney Wordsworth (Burgess Meredith) is declared 'obsolete' and sentenced to execution for the high crimes of reading books and having religious beliefs. Wordsworth doesn't intend to go quietly though and comes up with a cunning plan to discredit the state prosecutor (Fritz Weaver)...

The Obsolete Man is dramatically a bit pompous and dramatically obvious and one-sided but Burgess Meredith and Fritz Weaver are terrific as the two diametrically opposed foes and the sparse design of this episode is (when one considers the budgetary constraints that Twilight Zone operated under) very stylish and inventive in conveying this fascist future society. While there isn't much nuance to Serling's script and he's somewhat heavy handed it is nonetheless very satisfying to see Wordsworth turn the tables on Fritz Weaver and give the "Chancellor" a taste of his own medicine.

This is the sort of story that would definitely have outstayed its welcome if stretched out over an hour but it works well in this shorter 'classic' Twilight Zone format and is a relatively engrossing yarn from start to finish. The last act is quite clever and supplies some nice Twilight Zone style cosmic karma. Serling's tendency to occasionally gives actors overwritten monologues is sometimes in evidence here but one forgives Serling wearing his heart on his sleeve and the two lead actors are good enough to handle dialogue that might have sounded clunky in lesser hands (or mouths if you prefer). The Obsolete Man is an agreeably solid end to season two and pretty good on the whole. This is a solid mediation on the dangers of conformity and features a touching performance by Meredith. B+

The Third Season 1961/62

TWO (Director: Montgomery Pittman, Writer: Montgomery Pittman)

"This is a jungle, a monument built by nature honoring disuse, commemorating a few years of nature being left to its own devices. But it's another kind of jungle, the kind that comes in the aftermath of man's battles against himself. Hardly an important battle, not a Gettysburg or a Marne or an Iwo Jima. More like one insignificant corner patch in the crazy quilt of combat. But it was enough to end the existence of this little city. It's been five years since a human being walked these streets. This is the first day of the sixth year, as man used to measure time. The time? Perhaps a hundred years from now. Or sooner. Or perhaps it's already happened two million years ago. The place? The signposts are in English so that we may read them more easily, but the place is the Twilight Zone."

In the ruined aftermath of what appears to be World War III, two enemy soldiers (played by Charles Bronson and Elizabeth Montgomery respectively) encounter one another in a deserted and abandoned town. She is still ready to fight but he has had enough of war...

Two is a very interesting and quite compelling opening episode for series three. A deserted Hal Roach backlot makes for a believable (and at times surprisingly grim) post-apocalyptic setting and the two stars are superb in what is almost a silent production. Montgomery is suggested to be Russian and more impulsive and distrustful while Bronson's American soldier is tired of war and killing and willing to trust someone just to make a human connection.

Not an awful lot happens in Two but the little moments as the two combatants begin to form a bond of trust and peace are

rewarding and quietly moving and this works well enough as
an anti-war episode (happily, Two never comes across as
preachy or heavy-handed). This is an unusual episode that is
difficult to describe but it lulls you in with its rich and
desperate aura of sadness. These two characters are weary of
fighting and destruction. They just want to be normal people
again in a normal world. You wouldn't say that TWO is ever
quite elevated into a classic Twilight Zone episode but it's very
good for what it is and a fairly rewarding start to the third
season. B

The story is gritty and realistic (skeletal remains of humans
and animals) and strong on character. The beautiful Elizabeth
Montgomery would later become a big star in the sitcom
Bewitched but here she is completely different. Smudged in
mud with long brown hair, looking tired and rustic. She's great
- as is Bronson as the decent American soldier. His strong but
silent screen image is a perfect fit. The twist is that Bronson is
the pacifist and has to cope with the impulsive nature of the
more violent and moody Russian soldier who he merely wants
to be friends with. B

THE ARRIVAL (Director: Boris Sagal, Writer: Rod Serling)

"This object, should any of you have lived underground for the
better parts of your lives and never had occasion to look
toward the sky, is an airplane, its official designation a DC-3.
We offer this rather obvious comment because this particular
airplane, the one you're looking at, is a freak. Now, most
airplanes take off and land as per scheduled. On rare occasions
they crash. But all airplanes can be counted on doing one or
the other. Now, yesterday morning this particular airplane
ceased to be just a commercial carrier. As of its arrival it
became an enigma, a seven-ton puzzle made out of aluminum,
steel, wire and a few thousand other component parts, none of
which add up to the right thing. In just a moment, we're going

to show you the tail end of its history. We're going to give you
ninety percent of the jigsaw pieces and you and Mr Sheckly
here of the Federal Aviation Agency will assume the problem
of putting them together along with finding the missing pieces.
This we offer as an evening's hobby, a little extracurricular
diversion which is really the national pastime in the Twilight
Zone."

Grant Sheckly (Harold J Stone) is a brilliant aviation FAA
investigator who has never failed to get to the bottom of a
plane crash or incident. However, he now faces his greatest
challenge because Flight 107 has just successfully landed an an
airport with no passengers or crew onboard. The plane is
completely empty! How on earth did it manage to land then? A
puzzled Sheckly is now facing a mystery to rival the Mary
Celeste...

The Arrival is disappointing in the way that it presents us with
a fantastic mystery but then never quite works out what to do
for the ending and the explanation for said mystery. The
explanation feels underwhelming to say the least - almost as if
Rod Serling had no idea how to explain the wonderful mystery
we are presented with at the beginning of the story. It's a
shame really because this story promises so much in its early
scenes and does have some genuine moments of tension along
the way. The Arrival grabs our attention but then never quite
takes advantage of that by rewarding us with a memorable
third act.

It's fun though to see the ultra confident and usually peerless
Sheckly become increasingly frazzled by the puzzling events.
What really negates The Arrival as much as anything is the fact
that when one looks back at the story after the conclusion the
plotholes and things that don't make any sense suddenly
become very apparent. This story certainly had a lot of
potential but the end result is rather disappointing. The
solution to everything feels like a cop out and The Arrival
always seems somewhat flat and derivative of several (better)
Twilight Zone episodes like King Nine Will Not Return. Stone

is decent enough in the lead but Noah Keen and Fredd Wayne as supporting characters are required to supply just a little too much commentary and exposition. The Arrival never really makes any sense and proves to be underwhelming in the end after a good start. B-

THE SHELTER (Director: Lamont Johnson, Writer: Rod Serling)

"What you are about to watch is a nightmare. It is not meant to be prophetic, it need not happen, it's the fervent and urgent prayer of all men of good will that it never shall happen. But in this place, in this moment, it does happen. This is the Twilight Zone."

A group of friends are having a party to celebrate the birthday of Dr Bill Stockton (Larry Gates). These people are well-heeled and seemingly urbane and gentle. However, things change when a radio report suggests that a nuclear strike on the United States is imminent. It turns out that Dr Stockton is the only person in the street with his own nuclear bunker. Stockton insists he only has room and provisions for three people in his shelter - his wife (Peggy Stewart) and young son. His friends refuse to take no for an answer though and soon descend into panic and violence as they seek to force their way into Stockton's nuclear shelter...

The Shelter is quite a famous episode of The Twilight Zone but it sometimes tends to be dismissed as something of a clunker - or a missed opportunity at the very least. The main reason for this is that Serling is generally felt to have hammered home his point here in too obvious a fashion. The thesis of the episode is that civilisation is a precarious and fragile thing. It wouldn't take much to make people revert to more primal instincts and turn on one another. The argument against The Shelter is we are already aware of this concept. We all know that human beings have the capacity to be selfish and violent.

That said though The Shelter is at least quite gripping and it's fun to have a genuine element of nuclear paranoia in the show. At the time this episode was made the end of the Cold War was nowhere in sight and people had a very real fear of a World War III fought with atomic weapons. The actions of the characters in The Shelter do rather strain credibility at times but the episode is never boring and the juxtaposition of these people enjoying a genteel and happy birthday at the start to then descending into madness as they bicker and fight over the shelter is certainly stark and often compelling.

The acting is good (look out for Jack Albertson who played Charlie's Grandfather in Willy Wonka and the Chocolate Factory) and the story is always relatively gripping. This is sort of a companion piece to The Monsters Are Due On Maple Street. Very similar. Quiet suburbia transformed into an angry mob by mass collective fear, prejudice and panic. It's not as good as that episode though. The Shelter probably would have been insufferable in the end as an hour long episode but it works fairly well in the half hour format and the premise of the episode is compellingly dark. The Shelter definitely isn't perfect but it is worth watching and nowhere near as bad as it is sometimes portrayed to be. B

THE PASSERBY (Director: Elliot Silverstein, Writer: Rod Serling)

"This road is the afterwards of the Civil War. It began at Fort Sumter, South Carolina, and ended at a place called Appomattox. It's littered with the residue of broken battles and shattered dreams. In just a moment, you will enter a strange province that knows neither North nor South, a place we call the Twilight Zone."

As the Civil War rages on, Lavinia Godwin (Joanne Linville) resides in a ruined mansion and awaits news of her soldier husband. Confederate soldiers, injured and weary, trudge past as she waits...

The Passerby is a rather slow and odd episode. A folk song called Black Is The Color (Of My True Love's Hair) is used within the story and there's a fine dreamlike atmosphere as the soldiers trudge past the old house. Joanne Linville is pretty good as Lavinia and the design of the episode is quite impressive considering the constrictive budget Twilight Zone operated under. Here's the problem though. The rich atmosphere of The Passerby only goes so far. With hardly any story or plot to speak of and a twist that you will literally see coming from a mile off, The Passerby never builds on the foundations of its atmosphere and production to do anything especially surprising or interesting at all.

As a consequence of this, despite the inventive flourishes and impressive off-kilter ambience of the piece, The Passerby feels like a filler episode that is treading water.

One could probably forgive any viewer who ultimately found The Passerby rather dull in the end. This is not an episode that stays in the memory for very long or will feature too prominently in your list of episodes to rewatch. The Passerby is more of a mood piece than anything and your enjoyment will probably rest on how much you fall for the atmosphere. If you go in with lowish expectations you might enjoy this but it seems doubtful that The Passerby will be everyone's cup of tea. B-

A GAME OF POOL (Director: Buzz Kulik, Writer: George Clayton Johnson)

"Jesse Cardiff, pool shark, the best on Randolph Street, who will soon learn that trying to be the best at anything carries its own special risks in or out of the Twilight Zone."

Chicago pool hustler Jesse Cardiff (Jack Klugman) thinks he is the best and laments the fact that he never got a chance to prove this against the late pool ace Fats Brown (Jonathan Winters). As this is the Twilight Zone, Jesse's wish is granted and Fats magically appears to meet his challenge. The two men play a game of pool with high stakes indeed. If Jesse wins he will be regarded as the greatest ever. If he loses it will cost him his life...

Jack Klugman makes a welcome return to the show here and delivers another terrific performance. An episode where two people play pool doesn't sound tremendously exciting or interesting on the face of it but A Game of Pool is actually very absorbing and gripping and of course greatly enhanced by the good chemistry between Klugman and Jonathan Winters. The twist is satisfying and the episode is well directed with plenty of atmosphere and tension.

Fats is a great character because we see that he's very weary of his reputation and status. Getting to the top of a sport or profession is one thing but staying at the top is even more challenging and exhausting. There's always some new contender eager for a shot at the champ. The real test is not in becoming the best but remaining there when everyone wants to knock you off your perch. How do you cope with the expectation and pressure?

Jesse will experience some of this ennui for himself by the conclusion of the story. There's a rich supernatural atmosphere in this story that is very vivid and makes a nice spectral backdrop to the drama.

A Game of Pool is a strong Twilight Zone episode on the whole and definitely worth watching. A Game of Pool works because it isn't whimsical or light hearted as you might expect. It goes for realism rather than sentimentality. A nice meditation on the ramifications of winning and losing and being the best. A-

THE MIRROR (Director: Don Medford, Writer: Rod Serling)

"This is the face of Ramos Clemente, a year ago a beardless, nameless worker of the dirt who plodded behind a mule, furrowing someone else's land. And he looked up at a hot Central American sun and he pledged the impossible. He made a vow that he would lead an avenging army against the tyranny that put the ache in his back and the anguish in his eyes, and now one year later the dream of the impossible has become a fact. In just a moment we will look deep into this mirror and see the aftermath of a rebellion in the Twilight Zone."

A dictator named Ramos Clemente (Peter Falk) in Central America is told that a mirror will reveal the faces of those out to betray and kill him. Ramos becomes increasingly paranoid and frazzled as he attempts to cling onto power...

The great Peter Falk in a Twilight Zone! It's surely too good to be true isn't it? Well, sadly, yes, it is. The Mirror must be a candidate for the worst episode of The Twilight Zone ever made. Falk, in a preposterous fake beard, seems to be patterned on Castro and gives an eccentric performance in this tedious drama. One of the problems with this episode is that it - whatever the intentions - comes across as Serling having a pop at Castro and Cuba and presenting a one-sided story with no nuance at all. Maybe it might have been better if Ramos was a more generic character because there are always plenty of heartless dictators and regimes in the world much worse than Castro. To make Ramos so obviously a proxy for Castro seems odd.

The biggest cardinal sin of The Mirror though is to simply be dull. This episode, even at half an hour, is a real slog to get through. The setting, costumes, and accents are all hokey and unbelievable and everyone will guess the twist long before we get there. The Mirror is pretty awful on the whole. This is pure filler and hardly worth your time. It's a great shame indeed that they couldn't have found a better episode for Peter Falk to feature in. Serling's script here is Cold War heavy and merely reinforces the prejudices of the American public at the time (strange because Serling was usually a very liberal and enlightened writer). They obviously thought that Castro was some madman and murderer and the simplistic depiction of him is very superficial. Falk raves and struts to no great effect and is thoroughly wasted. D-

THE GRAVE (Director: Montgomery Pittman, Writer: Montgomery Pittman)

"Normally, the old man would be correct. This would be the end of the story. We've had the traditional shoot-out on the street and the badman will soon be dead. But some men of legend and folk tale have been known to continue having their way even after death. The outlaw and killer Pinto Sykes was such a person, and shortly we'll see how he introduces the town and a man named Conny Miller, in particular, to the Twlllight Zone."

In the Old West, bounty hunter Conny Miller (Lee Marvin) is mocked for his failure to capture outlaw Pinto Sykes - despite trailing him for a considerable time. Miller is annoyed that folks think he was scared of Pinto and deliberately chose not to confront him. Turns out that Pinto is dead now anyway. Pinto's last words were that if Miller ever visited his grave he would reach up and grab him. Miller is offered a wager by the men in the saloon. All he has to do is visit Pinto's grave at midnight and stick a knife in the burial mound to prove he was there...

The Grave is one of the better western themed Twilight Zones and a good solid ghost story (though ambiguity is used to good effect). Lee Marvin is terrific as Miller and is a well-rounded character in that he isn't Clint Eastwood in a spaghetti western but a very human character who is flawed and not immune to fear and doubt. The depiction of time and place is good here and I like the fact that this story seems to take place on a cold and windy night. This not a romantic depiction of the Old West and feels all the more authentic because of that.

It's great too to see Lee Van Cleef and James Best in the supporting cast. There is a great group of actors in this one. The challenge faced by Miller, that of visiting Pinto's grave at midnight, becomes very gripping and is fantastically atmospheric. The Grave is a little on the slow side at first but it gradually draws you into the premise and becomes more compelling as it goes on. While you wouldn't say this was an out and out classic The Grave is very solid and effective and does what it sets out to do very well. Despite the restrictive nature of the sets the western atmosphere well conveyed by the props men and the cast and the central task of Marvin's character gives The Grave is a good ghostly aura. This is a pretty good episode on the whole. A strength here is the source material by Montgomery Pittman. Pittman was excellent at detail and language, how people spoke in certain places and periods. B

IT'S A GOOD LIFE (Director: James Shelby, Writer: Rod Serling)

"Tonight's story on The Twilight Zone is somewhat unique and calls for a different kind of introduction. This, as you may recognize, is a map of the United States, and there's a little town there called Peaksville. On a given morning not too long ago, the rest of the world disappeared and Peaksville was left all alone. Its inhabitants were never sure whether the world was destroyed and only Peaksville left untouched or whether the village had somehow been taken away. They were, on the other hand, sure of one thing: the cause. A monster had arrived in the village. Just by using his mind, he took away the automobiles, the electricity, the machines - because they displeased him - and he moved an entire community back into the dark ages - just by using his mind. Now I'd like to introduce you to some of the people in Peaksville, Ohio. This is Mr Fremont. It's in his farmhouse that the monster resides. This is Mrs Fremont. And this is Aunt Amy, who probably had more control over the monster in the beginning than almost anyone. But one day she forgot. She began to sing aloud. Now, the monster doesn't like singing, so his mind snapped at her, turned her into the smiling, vacant thing you're looking at now. She sings no more.

And you'll note that the people in Peaksville, Ohio, have to smile. They have to think happy thoughts and say happy things because once displeased, the monster can wish them into a cornfield or change them into a grotesque, walking horror. This particular monster can read minds, you see. He knows every thought, he can feel every emotion. Oh yes, I did forget something, didn't I? I forgot to introduce you to the monster. This is the monster. His name is Anthony Fremont. He's six years old, with a cute little-boy face and blue, guileless eyes. But when those eyes look at you, you'd better start thinking happy thoughts, because the mind behind them is absolutely in charge. This is the Twilight Zone."

In the small town of Peaksville, everyone is terrified of six-year Anthony Fremont (Bill Mumy). Anthony has godlike powers and can do anything he wants simply by thinking about it. Not only that but he can read minds. Anyone who has an unhappy thought about him is liable to be turned into a jack-in-the-box and banished to the cornfield. Anthony has separated Peaksville from the world and blocked out television signals and electricity. No one is allowed to sing or listen to music because it displeases him. Everyone - even his parents - are scared to death of Anthony and must do everything he says for fear of punishment. Will the unhappy and captive population of Peaksville have the courage to act against Anthony and end this nightmare?

It's A Good Life (adapted from a story by Jerome Bixby) has a truly chilling premise that it uses to strong effect in one of the most famous Twilight Zone episodes. Imagine being at the mercy of a stroppy small boy who can turn you into an indescribable horror simply by thinking about it! Even when Anthony begins destroying precious dwindling crops by making it snow no one can tell him what he is doing is wrong for fear of provoking his anger. They must simply say - "That's a good thing you did Anthony! A good thing!" This line is laced with a subtext of desperation and hysteria that is truly terrifying.

The real tension comes here when Dan Hollis (Don keefer) gets drunk at his birthday on one of the few remaining bottles of alcohol left in the village and in his drunken state begins to complain about Anthony and tell him what he really thinks. We JUST know that poor old Dan is going to meet a horrible fate for his honesty. It's very tense too when Dan implores someone to do something - and by that he obviously means kill Anthony. But will anyone be brave enough to try? Failure will result in a dreadful retribution from the godlike boy. Anthony's mind-reading powers really increase the tension of the story. Don't think bad thoughts about him! It's A Good Life is enjoyably bleak and as scary as any Twilight Zone episode. This is really great stuff and justifies its reputation as one of the best known episodes in the history of the show. A

DEATHS-HEAD REVISITED (Director: Don Medford, Writer: Rod Serling)

"Mr Schmidt, recently arrived in a small Bavarian village which lies eight miles northwest of Munich, a picturesque, delightful little spot onetime known for its scenery but more recently related to other events having to do with some of the less positive pursuits of man: human slaughter, torture, misery and anguish. Mr Schmidt, as we will soon perceive, has a vested interest in the ruins of a concentration camp - for once, some seventeen years ago, his name was Gunther Lutze. He held the rank of a captain in the S.S. He was a black-uniformed strutting animal whose function in life was to give pain, and like his colleagues of the time he shared the one affliction most common amongst that breed known as Nazis: he walked the Earth without a heart. And now former S.S. Captain Lutze will revisit his old haunts, satisfied perhaps that all that is awaiting him in the ruins on the hill is an element of nostalgia. What he does not know, of course, is that a place like Dachau cannot exist only in Bavaria. By its nature, by its very nature, it must be one of the populated areas of the Twilight Zone."

"Mr Schimdt" (Oscar Beregi) arrives in a Bavarian village for a short stay. In reality, he is a former sadistic SS member named Captain Lutze who was notorious for his cruelty at Dachau concentration camp. Lutze takes a trip to the abandoned concentration camp and is nostalgic for the terrible power and authority he wielded there during the war.

A man named Becker (Joseph Schildkraut) appears at the camp and Lutze assumes he must be a caretaker. However, Becker is a former inmate of Dachau and is about to dispense some long overdue cosmic Twilight Zone karma for the indescribably evil crimes that Lutze committed...

Although Deaths-Head Revisited occasionally feels almost too important a subject for The Twilight Zone and is (unavoidably) rather grim at times, it works thanks to several mitigating factors. Serling's wraparound narrations are amongst his most poignant and heartfelt and Oscar Beregi is strong as the (at first) gleeful Nazi, nostalgic for the war and its attendant cruelty, wistfully remembering the time when a uniform gave him a great sense of power and importance. He's matched by Joseph Schildkraut as a former inmate named Becker who magically appears at Dachau to see that justice is done.

The set (which was a town set built for a western pilot) used for Deaths-Head Revisited is appropriately abandoned with a decent sense of scale and the dreamlike atmosphere forged by Don Medford is effective. The karma here is very satisfying.

Afterall, if a Nazi war criminal doesn't deserve a nightmarish trip to the Twilight Zone then who does? This episode could have come across as insensitive if handled incorrectly but it is beautifully directed, written, and performed and manages to avoid ever feel like something that borders on exploitation or bad taste. Deaths-Head Revisited, as it should be, is sensitive and sober and very moving. This was a brave idea for a Twilight Zone episode that come easily have come unstuck in lesser hands but thankfully it avoids the pitfalls that come with such a serious and weighty subject and becomes a very thoughtful and satisfying half hour of television. Serling's impassioned closing narration is rather moving. A-

THE MIDNIGHT SUN (Director: Anton Leader, Writer: Rod Serling)

"The word that Mrs Bronson is unable to put into the hot, still, sodden air is 'doomed,' because the people you've just seen have been handed a death sentence. One month ago, the Earth suddenly changed its elliptical orbit and in doing so began to follow a path which gradually, moment by moment, day by day, took it closer to the sun.

And all of man's little devices to stir up the air are now no longer luxuries - they happen to be pitiful and panicky keys to survival. The time is five minutes to twelve, midnight. There is no more darkness. The place is New York City and this is the eve of the end, because even at midnight it's high noon, the hottest day in history, and you're about to spend it in the Twilight Zone."

The Earth has deviated from its usual elliptical pathway and is gradually falling in its rotation towards the sun. It is now unbearably hot and getting hotter all the time. There is no more night. Only the blazing unbearable sun. Society has began to break down. There are water and food shortages. A young artist named Norma (Lois Nettleton) decides to stay in her apartment building but potential intruders and the intolerable heat threaten her safety...

One of the greatest Twilight Zone episodes ever made, The Midnight Sun uses a constrictive setting to weave a wonderfully compelling end of the world story and even conjures an outrageous twist ending in the bargain. Rod Serling proves to be well ahead of the curve in pondering the ecological fragility of the Earth and Lois Nettleton is terrific as Norma and allows the story to rest squarely on her shoulders. Bette Garde is also effective as her worried and elderly landlady Mrs Bronson.

The use of make-up to convey heat and humidity is excellent in The Midnight Sun - the characters believably looking as if they are caked in sweat and dehydrated at all times. Amazingly, this episode was shot in just three days. It's incredible really that something of this quality could be made so quickly. Though the production is low-budget and fairly static this story does a wonderful job in conveying a world that is coming to an end.

Atmosphere is conveyed by snippets of radio broadcasts and a sense that it's becoming more and more difficult to find out what is happening outside and in the wider world as a whole. You get a sense of society as we know it just starting to break and lose its cohesion offstage. There is some nice understated gallows humour here too at times.

There is a palpable sense of inevitable doom about the characters and situation in The Midnight Sun. The theme of this episode, that of mankind being insignificant and powerless in the face of greater forces like nature, fate, and an indifferent universe, is a classic Twilight Zone sort of scenario and beautifully cooked here to perfection.

The Midnight Sun is a brilliant episode. The story here has an enjoyable apocalyptic feel and constant air of impending disaster. You feel hot just watching. A

STILL VALLEY (Director: James Sheldon, Writer: Rod Serling)

"The time is 1863, the place the state of Virginia. The event is a mass blood-letting known as the Civil War, a tragic moment in time when a nation was split into two fragments, each fragment deeming itself a nation. This is Joseph Paradine, Confederate cavalry, as he heads down toward a small town in the middle of a valley. But very shortly, Joseph Paradine will make contact with the enemy. He will also make contact with an outpost not found on a military map - an outpost called the Twilight Zone."

Confederate scout Sergeant Joseph Paradine (Gary Merrill) finds a valley full of Union soldiers who all seem to be frozen in time. A mysterious old man named Teague (Vaughn Taylor) may hold the key to this mystery and the stakes could include Paradine's soul...

This episode was based The Valley Was Still by Manly Wade Wellman and feels like a filler sort of episode after three classic entries on the spin. The story here is never terribly interesting and while the frozen time concept is mildly arresting we've already had frozen time capers in The Twilight Zone before so Still Valley doesn't exactly score high marks for originality. This episode also has the same problem as Elegy in that the frozen people are obviously just extras and actors pretending to be frozen. You can see them wobbling slightly and trying desperately not to move or blink.

Still Valley also lacks the Civil War atmosphere of The Passerby. The performances in Still Valley are lively enough to mitigate some of the flaws but - alas - not all of them. Ultimately this a rather forgettable Twilight Zone episode that never really grabs your attention or lodges in the memory very much. Still Valley is by no means an out and out clunker but it is decidedly average and too often more of a chore than a pleasure to sit through. This is definitely one of those Twilight

Zones where you might find your attention starting to drift in places. Still Valley is ultimately rather derivative and disappointing. C+

THE JUNGLE (Director: William Claxton, Writer: Charles Beaumont)

"The carcass of a goat, a dead finger, a few bits of broken glass and stone, and Mr Alan Richards, a modern man of a modern age, hating with all his heart something in which he cannot believe and preparing, although he doesn't know it, to take the longest walk of his life, right down to the center of the Twilight Zone."

A wealthy engineer named Alan Richards (John Dehner) scoffs when he's told that a tribal curse has been placed on him because he oversaw a hydroelectric dam project in Africa which desecrated ancestral land. However, Richards is not scoffing anymore when the African curse seems to follow him back to the streets of New York...

The Jungle is a simple but effective little horror yarn with some nice moments of unease and atmosphere and a strong central turn by Dehner. There's some good direction when Richards walks through New York at night and the streets become increasingly lonely, strange and alive with the throbbing drums and animal noises of the jungle - in this case a very urban jungle! This is basically a spin on the voodoo story - a frequent staple in horror down the decades. The arc of Richards is good fun here because we see him go from doubting Thomas and sceptic to terror stricken over the course of the story.

Richards feels a lot like the sort of villain they would have in one of those EC Horror Comics. He didn't care about the traditions and rights of people in Africa. He simply wanted to get his dam built and pocket the money. For that he will of course pay the price of making a very unwelcome visit to the Twilight Zone. There's not an awful lot of plot in this story but it doesn't really matter. What this episode sets out to do it does well. It's atmospheric, quite creepy, and generally an entertaining and enjoyable half hour of horror anthology fun. Nice pay off at the end too. B

ONCE UPON A TIME (Director: Norman Z McLeod, Writer: Richard Matheson)

"Mr Mulligan, a rather dour critic of his times, is shortly to discover the import of that old phrase, 'Out of the frying pan, into the fire,' said fire burning brightly at all times in the Twilight Zone."

Woodrow Mulligan (Buster Keaton) is a janitor in 1890 who travels to the present day future thanks to a remarkable 'time helmet' a scientist has invented. Woodrow was unhappy in 1890 but finds the future is even worse and desires to go back to his own time. This proves to be a comically complex task though to say the least...

Once Upon a Time is a comedy episode that serves as an affectionate homage to the silent film era. The great Buster Keaton (who Matheson met and was determined to get on the show) is a delight and Stanley Adams lends decent support as Rollo (a man who quite fancies going back in time) but - while a nice idea - Once Upon A Time never really feels like The Twilight Zone and becomes a little tiresome in the end. The best parts of the film are constructed to mimic silent shorts from the heyday of Keaton. Some of his antics here are amazing considering his age as he runs around and falls off bicycles. It's a shame though that a long sequence in a repairman's shop rather sucks the energy and spirit out of the episode.

Buster Keaton, who was only five years away from his death

here, is still spry and enjoyable to watch onscreen but the antics over the time helmet never quite manage to sustain enough interest to make this anything especially noteworthy. The main problem with Once Upon a Time is that you do unavoidably end up wondering why you are watching an elderly Keaton go through his silent film shenanigans in a Twilight Zone episode when you can simply watch one of his classic films and shorts instead and get the undiluted authentic real thing (so to speak). It's fun and enjoyable to see the great Buster Keaton in Once Upon a Time but the episode itself is only average. It runs out of steam fairly soon and is not something you could see yourself returning to much but it is worth a watch just once to see Buster Keaton. C+

FIVE CHARACTERS IN SEARCH OF AN EXIT (Director: Lamont Johnson, Writer: Rod Serling)

"Clown, hobo, ballet dancer, bagpiper, and an army major - a collection of question marks. Five improbable entities stuck together into a pit of darkness. No logic, no reason, no explanation; just a prolonged nightmare in which fear, loneliness and the unexplainable walk hand in hand through the shadows. In a moment we'll start collecting clues as to the whys, the whats and the wheres. We will not end the nightmare, we'll only explain it - because this is the Twilight Zone."

Five strangers - Army Major (William Windom), Clown (Murray Matheson), Ballerina (Susan Harrison), Tramp (Kelton Garwood), and Bagpiper (Clark Allen) - find themselves trapped together in a metal cylinder with no memory of how they got there. How did they end up in here? Where are they? And more to the point, how do they escape?

This episode's title is a variation on the Pirandello play Six Characters in Search of an Author. Five Characters in Search of an Exit is an enjoyably offbeat and surreal Twilight Zone with a memorably bizarre get out of jail ending. The strangeness of the situation the characters find themselves in here is always interesting and the preposterous costumes merely add to the off-kilter aura. The always solid William Windom is well cast as the nominal lead (his army officer is the most determined to escape) and Murray Matheson adds to the claustrophobia with his nutty clown character.

Five Characters in Search of an Exit might ultimately be an exercise in frustration but it isn't an episode you'll forget in a hurry. The Spartan setting is in many ways the greatest strength of this episode in that the mystery is so perplexing and weird that you are immediately fascinated and curious to see what the explanation for this strange state of affairs is. The episode is at its most gripping when the characters (led by the army officer) make a determined attempt to escape. The twist at the end is so far out you can't help but just go along with it. Five Characters in Search of an Exit is a terrific little episode and up there with the most memorable Twilight Zone stories. A-

A QUALITY OF MERCY (Director: Buzz Kulik, Writer: Rod Serling)

"It's August, 1945, the last grimy pages of a dirty, torn book of war. The place is the Philippine Islands. The men are what's left of a platoon of American Infantry, whose dulled and tired eyes set deep in dulled and tired faces can now look toward a miracle, that moment when the nightmare appears to be coming to an end. But they've got one more battle to fight, and in a moment we'll observe that battle. August, 1945, Philippine Islands. But in reality it's high noon in the Twilight Zone."

In the last days of World War II in the Pacific, young Lieutenant Katell (Dean Stockwell) orders his men to assault a cave in which Japanese soldiers are holed up. The Japanese troops are already beaten for they are weak, starved, and trapped. The attack ordered by Katell seems unnecessary and it will undoubtedly come at the cost of the lives of some of his men. Katell's tired officers and men try to persuade him to call off the attack but he refuses to listen. The stubborn Katell is naturally about to take a trip to The Twilight Zone...

For some reason the World War 2 episodes of Twilight Zone were frequently slightly disappointing and A Quality of Mercy doesn't really manage to do much to alter that general perception. This episode is neither especially good or awfully bad or rather somewhere in the middle. Katell's encounter in the Twilight Zone forces him to look at things from another perspective and Serling seems a little too on the nose at times with his screenplay. Although the acting is good the make-up is unavoidably hokey looking (and perhaps a trifle racist to modern eyes) when Stockwell is made to look Japanese. Albert Salmi and a young Leonard Nimoy are also part of a very good ensemble cast. This story was shot on a jungle set at Hal Roach Studios and the fatigue and war weariness is convincing.

Serling served in World War 2 himself so was writing from experience. Maybe he experienced a young officer himself who came in and tried to make a name for himself by staging some suicidal attack - desperate to get something on his CV before the war ended. Serling's anti-war sentiments were very heartfelt and real but occasionally he could wear his heart on his sleeve a little too heavily in screenplays like this.

A Quality of Mercy has a great cast but the actual twist (and thus the device which gives the story its fantastical Twilight Zone tilt) is rather clunky and never terribly compelling. This is a very average episode on the whole despite the good work by the cast.

Albert Salmi as Causarano is sort of like Serling in this story, expressing the writer's own thoughts and view points. C+

NOTHING IN THE DARK (Director: Lamont Johnson, Writer: George Clayton Johnson)

"An old woman living in a nightmare, an old woman who has fought a thousand battles with death and always won. Now she's faced with a grim decision - whether or not to open a door. And in some strange and frightening way she knows that this seemingly ordinary door leads to the Twilight Zone."

Wanda Dunn (Gladys Cooper) is an old lady living alone in a dark tenement building that has been condemned and is due to be demolished. She hasn't opened her door for decades because she is terrified of "Mr Death". She believes that death can assume a variety of guises and that if she ever let someone in they might be death come to claim her. However, when a young policeman named Harold (Robert Redford) is shot in the snow outside her door he begs her to let him in and she has a big decision to make. Not only that but a Contractor (RG Armstrong) from the company due to stage the demolition of the building wants to get in too to talk to her. Wanda must make a decision on what to do with the injured policeman in the snow and confront her deepest fears...

Nothing in the Dark is a decent enough story about the unavoidable nature of death and our attitude to shuffling off this mortal coil at the end of life. This episode is quite moving at its best and has a dreamlike sort of quality. Stage actress Gladys Cooper affects a cockney accent here (which works better than that might sound) and it's her performance that gives Nothing in the Dark much of its gravitas and charm. Robert Redford is rather wooden in an early role here but it's not as if he ruins the episode or anything. He's decent enough.

This is a gentler sort of Twilight Zone story and has quite an uplifting quality by the end - despite the somewhat morbid and dark subject matter. You wouldn't say Nothing in the Dark was a classic but it's pretty good on the whole. Look out for RG

Armstrong too as a building contractor who is desperate to talk to Wanda because he's in charge of the demolition. This is all about fear of death but George Clayton Johnson suggests death is something that we should consider to be part of a natural process. Perhaps it comes with a gentle whisper and is merely the beginning and not the end. B

ONE MORE PALLBEARER (Director: Lamont Johnson, Writer: Rod Serling)

"What you have just looked at takes place three hundred feet underground, beneath the basement of a New York City skyscraper. It's owned and lived in by one Paul Radin. Mr Radin is rich, eccentric and single-minded. How rich we can already perceive; how eccentric and single-minded we shall see in a moment, because all of you have just entered the Twilight Zone."

The wealthy Paul Radin (Joseph Wiseman) invites three people - Mrs Langford (Katherine Squire), Reverend Hughes (Gage Clark), and Colonel Hawthorne (Trevor Bardette) - he feels have wronged him in the past to his New York skyscraper and tricks them into believing that an Atomic strike has occurred. Radin says they can all take refuge in his luxurious nuclear shelter on one condition. They must offer an apology for their actions. However, none of these guests are in the mood to give Radin Radin the apology he craves...

One More Pallbearer is an episode that promises more than it actually delivers. The premise is quite intriguing at the start but it soon becomes bogged down in a talky and rather dull story that soon begins to stretch our patience. The monologues are overwritten and it doesn't help that we have more sympathy for Radin than we do the three guests who refuse to apologise to him - which surely wasn't intentional?

Radin's guests value their pride and integrity more than their lives, which is of course admirable and brave, but for some reason they just come across as annoying in One More Pallbearer! This negates the core theme of the story. Joseph Wiseman (famously the first ever James Bond villain in 1962) is very watchable and crisp here as Radin but maybe makes the character too sympathetic in the end. One More Pallbearer also suffers from a rather preposterous double twist ending that will probably have you rolling your eyes and groaning. This episode is interesting at first but ends up disappointingly mediocre. By the way, I love the rather luxurious nuclear bunker that Radin has constructed! C+

DEAD MAN'S SHOES (Director: Montgomery Pittman, Writer: Charles Beaumont)

"Nathan Edward Bledsoe, of the Bowery Bledsoes, a man once, a spectre now. One of those myriad modern-day ghosts that haunt the reeking nights of the city in search of a flop, a handout, a glass of forgetfulness. Nate doesn't know it but his search is about to end, because those shiny new shoes are going to carry him right into the capital of the Twilight Zone."

Down and out Nathan Edward Bledsoe (Warren Stevens) takes some shoes from a dead gangster in an alley and finds himself controlled by the spirit of the deceased man. He is now compelled to extract revenge on a gangster boss...

Dead Man's Shoes is a fun little cartoonish noir gangster story that works well in black and white. The gangster stuff is a trifle hokey but it is entertaining. It's no classic but entertaining as far as it goes and apparently suffered from a lot of script changes in the transition from page to screen. With this in mind, Dead Men's Shoes is not bad at all. The noir atmosphere in this is decent fun with dark alleyways and gangster pads. Although this is not exactly the most dramatic and weighty episode of Twilight Zone ever made it helps that it's all played fairly straight. If this episode had been done as a light-hearted comedy caper it might well have ended up as insufferable but they strike a good balance here.

The basic premise is fun too (where else would one encounter haunted shoes but the Twilight Zone?) and mined pretty much to the hilt. You'll feel as if you got pretty good value by the end of this when it comes to haunted shoe capers. Dead Man's Shoes is not an especially important or classic episode of The Twilight Zone but it is fun and you should have a decent enough time watching this. Rewrites made the characters rather sketchy and inconsistent here but it's by no means a bad episode. If the shoe fits wear it goes the old saying. You should be very wary of that if Dead Man's shoes is anything to go by. B

THE HUNT (Director: Harold Schuster, Writer: Earl Hamner Jr)

"An old man and a hound dog named Rip, off for an evening's pleasure in quest of raccoon. Usually, these evenings end with one tired old man, one battle-scarred hound dog and one or more extremely dead raccoons, but as you may suspect that will not be the case tonight. These hunters won't be coming home from the hill. They're headed for the backwoods of the Twilight Zone."

Hyder Simpson (Arthur Hunnicut) is an old man in the South who loves nothing more than a ramble and bit of hunting in the woods with his beloved hound Rip. When Rip goes in the river after a raccoon and doesn't emerge, Hyder dives in after him and they both awake next to the water the following morning. When Hyder and Rip go home though they find that no one seems to acknowledge their presence. It seems they both died in the river. Do they let dogs in Heaven?

The Hunt is the first contribution to the series by Earl Hamner Jr - who was of course was later best known for creating the television series The Waltons. Hamner's scripts often featured rural country folk and The Hunt is certainly an example of that. Hamner often brought a whimsical backswoods sensibility and sense of humour to his Twilight Zone stories. The Hunt is often regarded to be a pretty terrible Twilight Zone episode but I don't actually think it's that bad. The central premise here - that Hyde refuses to enter Heaven unless his dog is allowed to go with him - is very sweet and makes the character likeable (which is no mean feat because Ryder is out hunting at the start - a pastime that you definitely wouldn't classify as sweet nor likeable).

This is a gentle whimsical sort of story with a relaxed sort of humour. Hunnicut's broad performance works in this context and although he's not exactly Laurence Olivier he's an engaging enough window through which to experience this story. The Hunt is pretty throwaway and forgettable compared to many other (superior) Twilight Zones but it passes the time and is always mildly interesting. Although not highly regarded in the pantheon of Twilight Zone episodes, The Hunt is certainly watchable and has a nice pay-off at the end. B-

SHOWDOWN WITH RANCE McGREW (Director: Christian Nyby, Writer: Rod Serling)

"Some one-hundred-odd years ago, a motley collection of tough moustaches galloped across the West and left behind a raft of legends and legerdemains, and it seems a reasonable conjecture that if there are any television sets up in cowboy heaven and any of these rough-and-wooly nail-eaters could see with what careless abandon their names and exploits are being bandied about, they're very likely turning over in their graves - or worse, getting out of them. Which gives you a clue as to the proceedings that will begin in just a moment, when one Mr Rance McGrew, a three-thousand-buck-a-week phoney-baloney discovers that this week's current edition of make-believe is being shot on location - and that location is the Twilight Zone."

Rance McGrew (Larry Blyden) is the star of a television western show. He is transported back in time to the Old West and discovers that the real Jesse James (Arch Johnson) isn't terribly happy about the way he is depicted in Rance's show...

Showdown with Rance McGrew is a tiresome episode that is mostly played for laughs with Larry Blyden delivering a ripe performance in the lead role. The premise, on paper at least, is sort of interesting. If a television cowboy star or action movie hero was put into a real life situation of the type they depict in their work then they'd probably turn out to be useless. Serling, rather acidly, once noted that John Wayne was constantly depicted as winning wars but did this on the safety of a Hollywood studio lot rather than a real combat theatre.

Sadly though, while this premise is interesting on paper it does not translate into a very good half hour of television - the jovial and unfunny comedic tone of the episode sinking it as much as anything. This is arguably the worst of Twilight Zones western themed episodes - which is a shame because the western themed Twilight Zones were often very watchable indeed. Showdown with Rance McGrew becomes a drag long before we reach the end. This is just a really boring episode and whatever Serling's intentions were they are lost here. Larry Blyden is not very funny or interesting in the lead despite his frantic efforts and hardly helps what is pretty much a lost cause of an episode. D

KICK THE CAN (Director: Lamont Johnson, Writer: George Clayton Johnson)

"Sunnyvale Rest, a home for the aged, a dying place, and a common children's game called kick the can that will shortly become a refuge for a man who knows he will die in this world if he doesn't escape into the Twilight Zone."

Charles Whitley (Ernest Truex) is a resident of Sunnyvale Rest Home for the elderly. When his son refuses to take him home he becomes depressed but decides that the secret to eternal youth is acting young. He begins to rouse the other residents into having fun but - most of all - he believes a game of "kick the can" will awaken memories of summers long past, freshly cut grass, and lost youth. Something magical might happen but he must persuade them to join him. The most obstinate though is his friend Ben (Russell Collins) who just thinks he's being an old fool...

Kick the Can is a very touching fable about old age and innocence with a heartwarming performance by Ernest Truex as the resident who has a profound impact on the lives of those who live in the home. The fantastical elements and the haunting music by Bernard Herrmann negate what could potentially have been a syrupy story with a wonderfully dreamlike coda and some strong supporting performances by the likes of Russell Collins as the obstinate Ben. Steven Spielberg remade this in the ill fated 1983 Twilight Zone Movie and failed miserably to extract the same simplicity of charm that is on show here.

Kick the Can is ultimately a wonderfully haunting and moving experience and probably the best of the many Twilight Zone episodes which revolved around older characters. There's real movie magic at play in those final scenes. This episode is a reminder of what a fantastically stylish and inventive show Twilight Zone could be at its best. Though the story might feel simple on the face of it, Kick the Can is a rich and very rewarding experience. The coda is the Twilight Zone at its most sublime and magical. This is a moving story about old age, death, youth and friendship with a good supporting cast and an excellent script. Maybe it takes a while to get into but it's definitely worth sticking with and shows The Twilight Zone at its best. A-

A PIANO IN THE HOUSE (Director: David Greene, Writer: Earl Hamner Jr)

"Mr Fitzgerald Fortune, theatre critic and cynic at large, on his way to a birthday party. If he knew what is in store for him he probably wouldn't go, because before this evening is over that cranky old piano is going to play 'Those Piano Roll Blues' with some effects that could happen only in the Twilight Zone."

A pompous drama critic Fitzgerald Fortune (Barry Morse) comes into the possession of a magical piano after buying it for his wife Esther's (Joan Hackett) birthday. The magic is rather dark though because the piano makes the player reveal their true selves and true thoughts. Esther reveals that she loathes her husband when she plays the piano. An embittered Fortune decides to throw a big party with the aim of humiliating his guests by having them play this most revealing piano...

A Piano in the House is watchable but never too much more than that. The theme is interesting enough though somewhat obvious. Who we appear to be the surface is not necessarily who we really are - or WANT to be be. There's often a disconnect between how we really see ourselves and how others see us because we create facades and personas in our public life. This episode becomes quite uncomfortable when Fortune's guests are made to reveal their true self - or at least the true self they really want to be.

One problem here is that the ending is rather predictable. We KNOW exactly where this story is going but then that's the ending we want anyway so it works reasonably well. The concept of a haunted piano is of course ridiculous and that's something this story is always grappling with but then this is the Twilight Zone so suspension of disbelief is already a given anyway. A lot of juice here is provide by Barry Morse and his fully committed and very watchable performance as the smug and cruel critic holds our attention. A Piano in the House is passable enough but not one of the more memorable Twilight

Zones when set against better entries in this show. B-

THE LAST RITES OF JEFF MYRTLEBANK (Director: Montgomery Pittman, Writer: Montgomery Pittman)

"Time, the mid-twenties. Place, the Midwest, the southernmost section of the Midwest. We were just witnessing a funeral, a funeral that didn't come off exactly as planned, due to a slight fallout from the Twilight Zone."

The supposedly dead Jeff Myrtlebank (Jeff Best) awakens in his open coffin during his funeral service and sets about going back to his life with fiancee Comfort (Sherry Jackson). However the locals are understandably rather wary of Jeff now...

The premise of The Last Rites of Jeff Myrtlebank make it sound like a pure horror yarn but it's actually a fairly whimsical bauble and quite agreeable on the whole. This is definitely one of those Twilight Zones though that was suited to the shorter format. I don't think the premise here would have fared so well if stretched over an hour. This was the first trip to the Twilight Zone for James Best and he's a likeable and charismatic presence as the lead here. Best would later be best known for The Dukes of Hazzard. He's very handsome and possessed of good comic timing in The Last Rites of Jeff Myrtlebank.

The intrigue here comes from the mystery of how Jeff cheated death and what changes it made to him. Is this the same Jeff Myrtlebank or a supernatural being? The locals are now rather fearful of him and ready to reach for their pitchforks and flaming torches. Some of the changes in Jeff are very obvious as he now has super strength and flowers wilt to his touch - which obviously makes any chance of picking things up again with Comfort complex to say the least. More than anything this episode is a love story - albeit a strange and off-kilter one. The Last Rites of Jeff Myrtlebank is no classic but it's perfectly watchable and not bad at all. This is a good episode with some nice performances and comic moments. Actually the Southern atmosphere is very Earl Hamner although he had nothing to do with this one. B

TO SERVE MAN (Director: Richard L Bare, Writer: Rod Serling)

"Respectfully submitted for your perusal: a Kanamit. Height: a little over nine feet. Weight: in the neighborhood of three hundred and fifty pounds. Origin: unknown. Motives? Therein hangs the tale, for in just a moment we're going to ask you to shake hands, figuratively, with a Christopher Columbus from another galaxy and another time. This is the Twilight Zone."

A race of alien beings known as Kanamits arrive on Earth and offer peace and new technology. The aliens even offer to set up an exchange programme whereby humans can visit the Kanamit home planet. But do these aliens have a hidden motive? The answer to that question may lie in a book the aliens left at the United Nations which is titled To Serve Man.

Cryptographers secretly beaver away at decoding the alien language so that they can translate the book...

Justifiably regarded to be one of the most memorable of any Twilight Zone episode, To Serve Man has a deliciously dark twist ending and compels from the start when we are introduced to cryptographer Michael Chambers (Lloyd Bochner) onboard a Kanamit spaceship. The story concerns the efforts of Earth's scientists and codebreakers to decipher a Kanamit document left at the UN building and this element is always a lot of fun as they scramble to work out if the alien visitors are harbouring secrets. Lloyd Bochner is suave as the solid lead but it's Richard Kiel who really steals the show as the Kanamit ambassador with a huge domed head prosthetic and flowing robes. He is downright weird looking with spaced out eyes and that unmistakable physical presence.

Kiel's scenes at the UN are very striking because he looks so out of place. Kiel plays all of the Kanamits you see in the episode and this tactic works quite well, giving them a creepy uniformity. At the time Kiel was shooting a famously bad (Mystery Science Theater 3000 lampooned) film called Eegah where he played a caveman. He was allowed to take a week off from the caveman shenanigans to shoot To Serve Man.

To Serve Man has a great atmosphere with the black and white and stunning music cues from Jerry Goldsmith. The alien saucer section in the episode is from Forbidden Planet and some stock footage from The Day the Earth Stood Still was used to depict the Kanamits arriving. The classic fifties sci-fi trappings are fun. Serling apparently insisted on reshoots after being unhappy with the initial cut and also inserted the flashback structure at a later date. His revisions obviously worked as this is considered to be a classic now. It all builds to the most oft-quoted line in Twilight Zone history and a darkly amusing coda by Rod Serling. To Serve Man is fantastic. A

THE FUGITIVE (Director: Richard L Bare, Writer: Charles Beaumont)

"It's been said that science fiction and fantasy are two different things: science fiction, the improbable made possible; fantasy, the impossible made probable. What would you have if you put these two different things together? Well, you'd have an old man named Ben who knows a lot of tricks most people don't know and a little girl named Jenny who loves him - and a journey into the heart of the Twilight Zone."

Ben (J Pat O'Malley) is a kind old fellow almost like a real life Father Christmas with his uncanny brand of magic. But Ben seems to be a wanted man and a little girl in his apartment block named Jenny (Susan Gordon) is determined to know why...

The Fugitive is a light relief episode in many ways but a very pleasant and likeable one nonetheless with British veteran J Pat O'Malley delightful as Old Ben and child actress Susan Gordon well cast as the curious Jenny. The staid apartment block atmosphere is well staged and gives the story a nicely prosaic backdrop from which to mount its flights of fancy. The Fugitive is rather predictable but it doesn't detract too much from an episode you'd have to be fairly cold hearted not to like.

There's quite a unique intro to this episode where Ben turns himself into a tree and then Rod Serling appears to do his opening monologue! While the premise here feels very familiar (it is a sturdy staple of science fiction) The Fugitive is warm hearted enough to justify its own existence and an enjoyable enough - if slight - sort of yarn. While I love the dark and scary episodes of Twilight Zone most of all it's nice too to have an episode that is simply gentle and nice. The Fugitive is no out and out classic but it is perfectly agreeable for what it is. The resolution is clever and despite being daft you go along with it all. Not a classic but The Fugitive is very charming all the same. B

LITTLE GIRL LOST (Director: Paul Stewart, Writer: Richard Matheson)

"Missing: one frightened little girl. Name: Bettina Miller. Description: six years of age, average height and build, light brown hair, quite pretty. Last seen being tucked in bed by her mother a few hours ago. Last heard - aye, there's the rub, as Hamlet put it. For Bettina Miller can be heard quite clearly, despite the rather curious fact that she can't be seen at all. Present location? Let's say for the moment in the Twilight Zone."

When his daughter Tina (Tracy Stratford) rolls under her bed one night and vanishes, Chris Miller (Robert Sampson) is bewildered as he can hear her calling out from somewhere in the room but can't find Tina anywhere. Equally strange is the fact that the family dog bolted after Tina under the bed and disappeared too. Chris and his wife Ruth (Sarah Marshall) summon family friend and physicist Bill (Charles Aidman) for help with this puzzling mystery and Bill listens to the distant cries (and barks!) for help and comes to a remarkable conclusion. He believes Tina has fallen through a hole into another dimension. The gateway must be somewhere near her bed. Will it be possible to follow Tina there and bring her safely back to our own reality?

The use of other dimensions or alternate realities in fictional entertainment is not exactly a new idea. Everyone from Lovecraft to Stephen King has used this device in stories. Dimensions, portals, and alternate realities have long been a staple of comics, movies, and anthology shows like The Twilight Zone and The Outer Limits. It is to the credit of Matheson here that he takes something we are very familiar with (too familiar you might argue) but still manages to make it feel fresh, intriguing, and mysterious.

Little Girl Lost is certainly above average with an interesting premise by Matheson and plenty of chills - not least the freaky deaky Fourth Dimension (made all the more surreal by Bernard Herrman's memorable score). The story doesn't really hold up to too much scrutiny (Chris, rather conveniently, is all too quick to consult physicist friend Bill rather than phone the police!) but this is well acted, well made and a mostly superior twenty-five minutes or so of television. By the way, Matheson apparently got the idea for this story when he heard his own daughter crying out one night but couldn't find her. It turned out she was under the bed. Little Girl Lost is a fun and very Twilight Zone sort of mystery and a terrific story on the whole.

Matheson seems to enjoy pitting this science boffin against

this pesky cosmic problem. Because we don't know what the fourth dimension is and no one has ever got a train there the writer was free to think about what it might be like in his own imagination. He therefore came up with the idea of a transient opening in the wall of Tina's bedroom where you can enter a strange warped world that doesn't conform to the laws of our own reality. What the story does do is wonderfully capture the spirit of The Twilight Zone - that is explore the great unknown and our fear of it. B+

PERSON OR PERSONS UNKNOWN (Director: John Brahm, Writer: Charles Beaumont)

"Cameo of a man who has just lost his most valuable possession. He doesn't know about the loss yet. In fact, he doesn't even know about the possession. Because, like most people, David Gurney has never really thought about the matter of his identity. But he's going to be thinking a great deal about it from now on, because that is what he's lost. And his search for it is going to take him into the darkest corners of the Twilight Zone."

David Gurney (Richard Long) wakes up one morning to - alarmingly - discover that he now seems to be a complete stranger to his friends and family. They all claim they've never seen him before in their life. Gurney must somehow prove who he really is and work out what is going on before they put him in the funny farm!

Loss of identity is a recurring theme in The Twilight Zone and one that was mined more than once to good effect. Person or Persons Unknown is one of the better spins at this well worn premise and Long's performance as Gurney is strong enough to make us feel the desperation of his plight and feel sympathetic towards him. The plight of Gurney to prove his real identity is not a delusion makes this episode rattle along at a decent clip and we are always engaged in the story. It's not quite what you would call a classic Twilight Zone episode but it is a very solid middle ranking sort of entry in the show.

The twist at the end is rather weird and quite good fun. Despite the very fantastical premise there's a strangely convincing sort of realism in this episode in that if a complete stranger came up to you and claimed to be a friend or relative your reaction would probably be of polite indifference - you'd simply want to get rid of them. That's the reaction the increasingly frazzled Gurney receives from those who he thought were closest to him. This theme is always interesting and rather chilling too. Person or Persons Unknown is perfectly watchable on the whole and a fairly entertaining half hour of television. The only possible criticism really is that it's similar to a Richard Matheson episode called A World of Difference but these types of stories are quintessential Twilight Zone fodder and always enjoyable if played right. B

THE LITTLE PEOPLE (Director: William Claxton, Writer: Rod Serling)

"The time is the space age, the place is a barren landscape of a rock-walled canyon that lies millions of miles from the planet Earth. The cast of characters? You've met them: William Fletcher, commander of the spaceship; his copilot, Peter Craig. The other characters who inhabit this place you may never see, but they're there, as these two gentlemen will soon find out. Because they're about to partake in a little exploration into that gray, shaded area in space and time that's known as the Twilight Zone."

Bickering astronauts William Fletcher (Claude Akins) and Peter Craig (Joe Maross) are marooned on an asteroid and must repair their rocket ship. One day, Craig discovers a tiny advanced civilisation on the asteroid smaller than ants. Delighted with the power his size gives him over this tiny world, the increasingly insane Craig is soon playing god to these unfortunate little people...

The Little People is an enjoyable (pardon the pun) little episode with Serling's rumination on the highly dangerous combination of ego and human nature left unchecked wrapped up in vintage sci-fi trappings with the Star Trek-ish asteroid surface stagebound but fun all the same. Akins and Maross are good value even if their characters are rather one-dimensionally good/bad to provide the confrontation the story needs. Atkins is the straight arrow captain who just wants to repair the ship while Maroos (clearly enjoying himself) is allowed to chew the scenery as the increasingly deranged Craig. "All right, my little friends, comes now the new age, the age of... the age of Peter Craig! Let us commence to build the statue again, let us commence to begin!"

Maross has fun as the deranged and oleaginous Craig, who quickly goes bonkers when he finds the tiny race of people, eager to make them fear him and cater to his every whim. The decent Fletcher tells Craig they should leave the race of tiny people in peace and concentrate on getting off the asteroid but the arrogant Craig becomes drunk with the power his size gives him over this microscopic civilisation. He's soon lording it over the miniature world, telling them they have a new god, threatening destruction, and ordering a huge statue of himself to be constructed in the city. He decides he's going to stay here bossing them around whether Fletcher likes it or not.

The microscopic society is hinted at more than conveyed (there is use of stock footage of boats, cars etc. when Craig takes a magnified look) but those high pitched squeaks of commotion from down below are fun anyway. The twist ending of The Little People is preposterous but great fun all the same and very satisfying. This episode doesn't seem to have an especially lofty reputation when it comes to The Twilight Zone but personally it's one that I've always had a lot of fun with myself. The Little People is an episode I always include whenever I do a Twilight Zone marathon and always have a good time when I return to it. The Little People was shot in Death Valley and rife with atmosphere. The rocky, lonely asteroid, the rocket ship silent and awaiting repair, and the strange little world that Craig discovers. The beeps and metallic shudders of the ailing ship, ominous music, and then the high-pitched chatter of the tiny city. B+

FOUR O'CLOCK (Director: Lamont Johnson, Writer: Rod Serling)

"That's Oliver Crangle, a dealer in petulance and poison. He's rather arbitrarily chosen four o'clock as his personal Gotterdammerung, and we are about to watch the metamorphosis of a twisted fanatic, poisoned by the gangrene of prejudice, to the status of an avenging angel, upright and omniscient, dedicated and fearsome. Whatever your clocks say, it's four o'clock, and wherever you are it happens to be the Twilight Zone."

Oliver Crangle (Theodore Bikel) is a self-appointed moral guardian who causes great anguish by writing endless letters of complaint and staging telephone calls to people he is offended by. He believes, through a great act of willpower, that he will make all the wrongdoers in the world shrink at 4 O'Clock...

Four O'Clock, sadly, turns out to be a complete dud in the end. This is an episode that never goes anywhere in particular and the ending is so predictable that you'll guess where this is going long before we actually get there. It's hard to know exactly what the point of this one-sided and obvious story is. It could be perhaps that Serling's subtext is the McCarthy Witch Hunts.

Crangle is also basically a conspiracy theorist. He thinks that communists, murderers, and various other groups are engaged in a conspiracy to take over Washington. Conspiracy theorists generally have to operate on the fringes of public discourse and are often (for good reason) dismissed as crackpots, cranks, and racists. Too often they wander down the red herring anti-Semitic rabbit hole of what is commonly known as the Jewish banker conspiracy (the most famous proponent of this conspiracy theory was of course Hitler). It could be then that Serling's script here also has a subtext about anti-Semitism.

Four O'Clock basically consists of Theodore Bikel as Crangle in his room becoming increasingly deranged and hammy. This is interesting at first but then the static and talky nature of the piece becomes tiresome. The idea of course is that Crangle is the evil one - not the people he is targeting and persecuting. This is definitely not an episode you'll be returning to in a hurry. D+

HOCUS POCUS AND FRISBY (Director: Lamont Johnson, Writer: Rod Serling)

"The reluctant gentleman with the sizeable mouth is Mr Frisby. He has all the drive of a broken camshaft and the aggressive vinegar of a corpse. As you've no doubt gathered, his big stock in trade is the tall tale. Now, what he doesn't know is that the visitors out front are a very special breed, destined to change his life beyond anything even his fertile imagination could manufacture. The place is Pitchville Flats, the time is the present. But Mr Frisby's on the first leg of a rather fanciful journey into the place we call the Twilight Zone."

Mr Frisby (Andy Devine) runs the local store and is famous for making up remarkable (and patently exaggerated and untrue) stories about himself. But alien visitors with no concept of lying believe everything he says and make plans to kidnap Frisby to keep as a specimen in an extraterrestrial zoo...

While a very middle ranking Twilight Zone episode that is

easily forgotten, Hocus-Pocus and Frisby is better than some of Serling's other lighter comedic screenplays thanks mainly to the injection of aliens into the story (their cramped spaceship interiors and bandaged faces are both creepy and fun) and the presence of William Devance as the compulsive liar Frisby. Devane has a very distinctive voice that feels perfect for Frisby and it's a measure of his skill here that he plays a grating blowhard liar like this and yet we still root for him.

Hocus-Pocus and Frisby is pretty silly stuff but it is quite entertaining and the central premise of an armchair liar making up extraordinary things and THEN having an extraordinary adventure for real is sort of fun. This episode could easily have been terrible and insufferable but the end result is not that bad at all and surprisingly watchable. The injection of some sci-fi into the story gives it a boost I think. A whole episode of Devine in his store spinning tall tales might have outstayed its welcome rather quickly. B-

THE TRADE-INS (Director: Elliot Silverstein, Writer: Rod Serling)

"Mr and Mrs John Holt, ageing people who slowly and with trembling fingers turn the last pages of a book of life and hope against logic and the preordained that some magic printing press will add to this book another limited edition. But these two senior citizens happen to live in a time of the future where nothing is impossible, even the trading of old bodies for new. Mr and Mrs John Holt, in their twilight years, who are about to find that there happens to be a zone with the same name."

In the future, elderly couple John (Joseph Schildkraut) and Marie (Alma Platt) visit The New Life Corporation - a company that has the technology to transplant your consciousness into a new, young body. But John and Marie only have enough money for one of them to start a new life...

The Trade-Ins is a decent enough episode and Serling's ponderings on how body modification might be an everyday occurrence through medical science in the future are always interesting. The Trade-Ins has a somewhat outlandish premise but, generally, we get the strong impression that Serling is glad he wouldn't have to live in a time where it's so easy for people to alter their appearance they sometimes don't even seem like themselves anymore.

Schildkraut and Platt are fine as the leads and the contrast between this old fashioned and fragile couple make the clinical and sleek New Life Corporation feel all the more unnatural and sinister. You'll probably guess how this all ends but it's a sweet and thoughtful little Twilight Zone story that is well played by the cast. I suppose one could say this episode is about ageing gracefully more than anything. The relationship between the old couple in this is rather touching and so makes The Trade-Ins a likeable and gently moving episode. There is a major gap in the logic of this story but it's a sweet episode that is always very watchable. B-

THE GIFT (Director: Allen H Miner, Writer: Rod Serling)

"The place is Mexico, just across the Texas border, a mountain village held back in time by its remoteness and suddenly intruded upon by the twentieth century. And this is Pedro, nine years old, a lonely, rootless little boy, who will soon make the acquaintance of a traveller from a distant place. We are at present forty miles from the Rio Grande, but any place and all places can be the Twilight Zone."

While crash-landing near a Mexican village, a human looking alien who calls himself Williams (Geoffrey Horne) accidentally kills a police officer. He stumbles into the village where he collapses in a bar and is treated by a kind doctor. Williams befriends a boy named Pedro (Edmund Vargas) and gives him

a book. He says he will explain the explain the significance of
the book later and that it is very important. But a bartender
has alerted the authorities to the presence of Williams and he
is now a wanted man...

The Gift is a perfectly dreadful Twilight Zone episode and
easily one of the dullest in the history of the show. The cast are
uniformly wooden and the Mexican stereotypes are hokey and
borderline offensive. The twist at the end is hardly worth the
tedious slog it takes to get there. The story has some obvious
themes about our distrust of outsiders and the need to be more
open and trusting but a problem here is that this alien fugitive
type of story has been done to death too many times.

This sort of story can still work if done quite well (The
Fugitive, as we noted, was a likeable and watchable episode)
but The Gift feels one of those scripts that found Serling in an
uninspired frame of mind and was stuck at the bottom of a
drawer gathering dust and plucked out simply because they
needed something to film that week.

The Gift, whatever its good intentions, commits the worst sin
of any Twilight Zone episode in that it is simply boring. This is
not an episode that you'll feel compelled to return to the
future. Geoffrey Horne and the Mexican boy who plays Pedro
are both pretty awful in this. The Gift is only of note really for
the music by Spanish composer and guitarist Laurindo
Almedia. D

THE DUMMY (Director: Abner Biberman, Writer: Rod Serling)

"You're watching a ventriloquist named Jerry Etherson, a
voice-thrower par excellence. His alter ego, sitting atop his lap,
is a brash stick of kindling with the sobriquet 'Willy.' In a
moment, Mr Etherson and his knotty-pine partner will be
booked in one of the out-of-the-way bistros, that small, dark,

intimate place known as the Twilight Zone."

Drunken ventriloquist Jerry Etherson (Cliff Robertson) becomes increasingly paranoid that his dummy Willy is sentient and out to get him. Is this merely a delusional figment of Jerry's sozzled imagination or does Willy really have a mind of his own?

The synopsis sounds very familiar and has been done previously and subsequently numerous times (most successfully in the 1945 Ealing horror film Dead of Night) but The Dummy is strong enough to stand on its own two feet and has a typically strong performance by Cliff Robertson (happily back in the Twilight Zone again) as the alcoholic ventriloquist. The puppet is suitably creepy and there are some memorable images and scares.

The depiction of the smoke hazed cabaret entertainment world that Jerry inhabits is nicely conveyed and the battle of wills between him and his creepy dummy becomes compellingly twisted and engaging. I quite like the fact that if you knew nothing about this episode you wouldn't think it is going to be a dark scary one at first but it does become an effective spine tingling drama when Jerry begins to become convinced that Jerry is alive and has dark intentions towards him. The twist at the end is enjoyably dark and weird and all in all this is one of the memorable of Twilight Zone's horror tinged episodes. It's to the great credit of the show here that they took an idea which had already been done before but still managed to do it well enough to make The Dummy justify its own existence and stand as a great little thriller in its own right. B+

YOUNG MAN'S FANCY (Director: John Brahm, Writer: Richard Matheson)

"You're looking at the house of the late Mrs Henrietta Walker. This is Mrs Walker herself, as she appeared twenty-five years ago. And this, except for isolated objects, is the living room of Mrs Walker's house, as it appeared in that same year. The other rooms upstairs and down are much the same. The time, however, is not twenty-five years ago but now. The house of the late Mrs Henrietta Walker is, you see, a house which belongs almost entirely to the past, a house which, like Mrs Walker's clock here, has ceased to recognize the passage of time. Only one element is missing now, one remaining item in the estate of the late Mrs Walker: her son, Alex, thirty-four years of age and, up till twenty minutes ago, the so-called perennial bachelor. With him is his bride, the former Miss Virginia Lane. They're returning from the city hall in order to get Mr Walker's clothes packed, make final arrangements for the sale of the house, lock it up and depart on their honeymoon. Not a complicated set of tasks, it would appear, and yet the newlywed Mrs Walker is about to discover that the old adage 'You can't go home again' has little meaning in the Twilight Zone."

A bachelor named Alex Walker (Alex Nicol) is finally about to get married to Virginia (Phyllis Thaxter). Alex was dominated by his possessive mother but now that she's passed on he plans to sell her home and start a new life. On visiting his childhood home though Alex is overwhelmed by nostalgia and feelings for his late mother and begins to have second thoughts about selling the house. Virginia begins to suspect that the late Mrs Walker is interfering in their affairs from beyond the grave...

Considering this is a Richard Matheson penned ghost story, Young Man's Fancy is fairly disappointing and run of the mill with the cliched creepiness of chiming clocks and radios with a life of their own soon wearing thin. Matheson himself was apparently quite unhappy with this episode and felt it didn't do his story justice. The cast are decent enough but ultimately this episode never quite grabs you in the way that the best Twilight Zone episodes do and is ultimately rather forgettable.

The twist is ok but this is not an episode you'll find yourself pining to return to in a hurry. Matheson intended this story to be much scarier and darker than it actually plays out on the screen here. Young Man's Fancy is not an out and out clunker but it is rather bland in the end and feels like it could have been much better. There is a decent twist at the end here and it sort of works as a ghost story and rumination on never escaping from one's past but ultimately this is fairly ordinary C+

I SING THE BODY ELECTRIC
(Director: James Sheldon and William Claxton, Writer: Ray Bradbury)

"They make a fairly convincing pitch here. It doesn't seem possible, though, to find a woman who must be ten times better than mother in order to seem half as good, except, of course, in the Twilight Zone."

A single dad (played by David White) buys a charming android grandmother (Josephine Hutchinson) to help look after his three children. However, young Anne (Veronica Cartwright) refuses to accept this robot granny because she's still grieving over the death of their mother and is frightened of becoming close to her new guardian lest she should suffer another loss...

This was Ray Bradbury's only contribution to The Twilight Zone but sadly it isn't one of the great episodes. Apparently, the reason why Bradbury didn't contribute more stories to the show is that Rod Serling, though a big Bradbury fan, felt his work was hard to adapt for the screen and often too elaborate for the limited budgets of the show. I Sing the Body Electric is a fairly sweet and pleasant episode that (perhaps unfairly) is judged rather too critically because it marked the only pairing of Ray Bradbury and The Twilight Zone.

The story never makes an awful lot of sense (robot granny indeed!) but Josephine Hutchinson is delightful and Veronica Cartright (who would of course feature in Ridley Scott's Alien as an adult) is good too as the child who is resistant to their new grandmother at first. The other child actors in this are pretty awful though and not terribly well cast. This episode was apparently reshot a couple of times because they thought the early efforts were unwatchable. This final version is not exactly brilliant so heaven knows how bad the others were. The syrup is ladled on unsparingly but I Sing the Body Electric is ok as far as it goes. The ending is pleasantly uplifting. B-

CAVANDER IS COMING (Director: Christian Nyby, Writer: Rod Serling)

"Submitted for your approval, the case of one Miss Agnes Grep, put on Earth with two left feet, an overabundance of thumbs and a propensity for falling down manholes. In a moment she will be up to her jaw in miracles, wrought by apprentice angel Harmon Cavender, intent on winning his wings. And, though, it's a fact that both of them should have stood in bed, they will tempt all the fates by moving into the cold, gray dawn of the Twilight Zone."

Accident prone eccentric usherette Agnes Grep (Carol Burnett) is visited by guardian angel Cavander (Jesse White) - who is determined to change her life...

Shades of Mr Bevis as Cavander Is Coming was floated as a potential pilot for a new comedy show and (believe it or not) originally screened with canned laughter. The laughter track is (mercifully) removed these days and rightly so as Cavander is Coming isn't amusing in the slightest. Serling fashioned this as a vehicle for Carol Burnett but she clearly doesn't have the faintest idea what is going on in this episode and you can hardly blame her. Burnett is likeable and full of energy but she's fighting a losing battle with this screenplay.

Cavender Is Coming is an absolute clunker and feels completely out of place as a Twilight Zone episode. This is arguably the worst of Twilight Zone's mixed bag of comic episodes and guardian angel shenanigans have by this stage in the show become rather tiresome. Cavender Is Coming feels like a complete waste of time for all involved - not least the poor viewer and any dedicated Twilight Zone completist who sits through this. Cavender Is Coming is rather boring really - which is the greatest sin of any Twilight Zone episode to transmit to the viewer. D

THE CHANGING OF THE GUARD (Director: Robert Ellis Miller, Writer: Rod Serling)

"Professor Ellis Fowler, a gentle, bookish guide to the young, who is about to discover that life still has certain surprises, and that the campus of the Rock Springs School for Boys lies on a direct path to another institution, commonly referred to as the Twilight Zone."

A veteran teacher named Professor Fowler (Donald Pleasance) is distraught and suicidal when he is told he has to retire after fifty years of teaching. He wonders if he made any impression on all on the many pupils who came and went over the decades. Professor Fowler will find the answer to that question in the Twilight Zone...

After rather too many underwhelming episodes in the back end of season three, we at least end on a high note with The Changing of the Guard. This is most notable for a beautiful performance from Donald Pleasance as the kind old teacher concerned about his legacy. "They come and go like ghosts. Faces, names, smiles, the funny things they said or the sad things, or the poignant ones. Poetry that left their minds the minute they themselves left. Aged slogans that were out of date when I taught them. I moved nobody. I motivated nobody."

The Changing of the Guard plays sort of like a ghostly Twilight Zone version of Dead Poet's Society and I love the winter bound anachronistic school. They had to put old age make-up on Pleasance to make him look like an old man but both he and the make-up are convincing enough to give the character authenticity. Pleasance apparently only had a few days to prepare for this role so his performance is all the more impressive. The Changing of the Guard is touching final episode for this season and nicely directed. This is a lovely and moving way to end the third year. B+

The Fourth Season 1962

IN HIS IMAGE (Director: Perry Lafferty, Writer: Charles Beaumont)

"What you have just witnessed could be the end of a particularly terrifying nightmare. It isn't. It's the beginning. Although Alan Talbot doesn't know it, he is about to enter a strange new world, too incredible to be real, too real to be a dream. It's called the Twilight Zone."

A man named Alan Talbot (George Grizzard) is troubled by some unsettling experiences which culminate in a visit to his home town where his past, his memories and his very existence seem to have been erased...

Twilight Zone was late in arranging a sponsor for year four so CBS replaced the show for a series called Fair Exchange. Fair Exchange was cancelled though so Twilight Zone was brought back. However, in order to fill the new time slot, Twilight Zone was expanded to one hour. The expanded running time was something of a mixed blessing (anthology shows tend to work best in half hour slots) and Twilight Zone returned to the half hour format for the fifth and final season.

The hour long Twilight Zone season is sometimes regarded to be much weaker than the half hour seasons but this is slightly unfair because there are some terrific stories in the fourth season. However, when an episode doesn't work one definitely notices it much more simply because you have an extra half hour or so of a dud episode to sit through!

In His Image is among the strongest of the hour long Twilight Zones and makes for a compelling opening to season four. The episode begins in arresting fashion when Talbot is accosted on the subway by a religious fanatic who won't leave him alone and keeps trying to thrust a leaflet in his hand. Suddenly hearing strange noises in his head, Talbot snaps and pushes her in front of a speeding train. An hour later, he arrives at the home of his finance Jessica Connelly (Gail Kobe) with no memory whatsoever of the murder he has just committed.

Talbot is taking Jessica to his home town of Coeurville to visit his Aunt Mildred. When they reach Coeurville though Talbot is in for a big shock. There are many brand new buildings he doesn't recognise, his key doesn't fit the lock of Aunt Mildred's door and a stranger answers and says he is unaware of anyone called Mildred ever living there. The university where Talbot works is an empty field and his parents' graves are gone - replaced by the tombstones of people he's never heard of before.

The mystery is developed in compelling fashion and there are twists galore when the reveals arrive. While the hour long format was a problem for many of the episodes in season four and made them feel padded and long winded, In His Image successfully maintains the intrigue and suspense over the duration of its running time and always holds your attention.

Talbot's unsettling experience of finding his home town changed beyond all recognition (in what seems an impossibly short space of time) is merely the first of a series of big twists and revelations that send the episode heading towards a cliff-hanger final act.

George Grizzard is terrific as Talbot and has to deploy a lot of skill as an actor as the story progresses. Gal Kobe is superb too as Jessica. Her responses to are always believable and she never allows her character to slide into hysteria. The only flaw one might suggest here is we've already seen this type of loss of identity story in the show before (and more than once too!) but In His Image is good enough to justify its own existence and a fine start to season four. B+

THE THIRTY-FATHOM GRAVE
(Director: Perry Lafferty, Writer: Rod Serling)

"Incident one hundred miles off the coast of Guadalcanal. Time: the present. The United States naval destroyer on what has been a most uneventful cruise. In a moment, they're going to send a man down thirty fathoms and check on a noise maker - someone or something tapping on metal. You may or may not read the results in a naval report, because Captain Beecham and his crew have just set a course that will lead this ship and everyone on it into the Twilight Zone."

A US Navy destroyer on patrol near Guadalcanal picks up an unexplained and mysterious clanking noise coming from the bottom of the sea. Captain Beecham (Simon Oakland) decides to deploy the ship's deep sea diver McClure (John Considine) to investigate. The mystery becomes even spookier when a crew member named Chief Bell (Mike Kellin) starts to exhibit paranoid and hysterical behaviour...

A slightly underrated Twilight Zone episode, The Thirty-Fathom Grave is actually a lot of fun and has a great atmosphere. It only really suffers from the extended running time - the story stretched out more than it needed to be. The first deep sea dive to the bottom of the sea is enjoyable and eerie but after this is repeated more than once our patience understandably begins to be tested. There is definitely a detectable element of padding to the story here in deference to the expanded running time Twilight Zone now has to fill. The Thirty-Fathom Grave probably would have worked much better as a half hour Twilight Zone story.

The cast is good (Simon Oakland ever dependable and sturdy as the captain and look out for Incredible Hulk star Bill Bixby as one of the crew) and although the ending might be predictable it's effective enough. The Thirty-Fathom Grave is

just a good fun nautical ghost story and it's enjoyable to have a
Twilight Zone story set at sea. I suspect that in the half hour
format this episode might be regarded to be a minor classic
but the hour long format does diminish it slightly.

The Thirty-Fathom Grave is not quite at the top table of
Twilight Zone episodes but is a solid nautical ghost story that
is better than its general reputation would suggest. Stephen
King actually gave this a mention as one of his favourite
episodes in his non-fiction book Danse Macabre. It's always
enjoyably creepy when the metallic thumps begin again from
beneath the waves, sounding exactly like someone
methodically tapping on a metal door with a hammer from the
inside. B

VALLEY OF THE SHADOW Director: (Perry Lafferty, Writer: Charles Beaumont)

"You've seen them. Little towns, tucked away far from the
main roads. You've seen them, but have you thought about
them? What do the people in these places do? Why do they
stay? Philip Redfield never thought about them. If his dog
hadn't gone after that cat, he would have driven through
Peaceful Valley and put it out of his mind forever. But he can't
do that now, because whether he knows it or not, his friend's
shortcut has led him right into the capital of the Twilight
Zone."

Phillip Redfield (Ed Nelson) is a journalist on his way to New
Mexico for an assignment. Out of gas, he stops off at a small
out of the way town called Peaceful Valley where everyone
seems a bit odd and wary of him. It turns out that the
inhabitants of Peaceful Valley are in secret possession of
remarkable technology and when Redfield accidentally
becomes aware of that technology he is told that he can never
leave the town again lest he should divulge the secrets of
Peaceful Valley to the outside world...

Valley of the Shadow is a somewhat middle of the road Twilight Zone episode - neither great nor poor but entertaining enough (although, once again, the longer running time sometimes feels too much). The premise is always interesting and the use of teleportation technology seems to anticipate Gene Roddenberry's Star Trek - which is ironic because James 'Scotty' Doohan is among the cast members. Ed Nelson is fine in the lead but if one had a criticism it would be that the town appears to be almost empty and very anachronistic. If the residents of Peaceful Valley were run by a cabal possessed of remarkable technology then the town would surely not look like something out of the Old West?

The reverse effects for the atomic disassembly/reassembly devices are generally well done and Valley of the Shadow is certainly intriguing in its early scenes. I'm always a sucker for stories like this where someone becomes trapped in a strange out of the way town or village. David Opatoshu adds some gravitas as Dorn, the chief town elder, and the explanation for the technology is enjoyably outlandish and very much in the spirit of Twilight Zone. I rather like this episode on the whole but it definitely loses a star by being dragged out to an hour. It just feels too long in the end. B-

HE'S ALIVE (Director: Stuart Rosenberg, Writer: Rod Serling)

"Portrait of a bush-league fuehrer named Peter Vollmer, a sparse little man who feeds off his self-delusions and finds himself perpetually hungry for want of greatness in his diet. And like some goose-stepping predecessors he searches for something to explain his hunger, and to rationalize why a world passes him by without saluting. That something he looks for and finds is in a sewer. In his own twisted and distorted lexicon he calls it faith, strength, truth. But in just a moment Peter Vollmer will ply his trade on another kind of corner, a strange intersection in a shadowland called the Twilight Zone."

Peter Vollmer (Dennis Hopper) is the leader of a small group of American neo-Nazis and gives what are meant to be rabble rousing speeches on street corners but is only met by jeering and ridicule. One night, Vollmer (Dennis Hopper) conjures the spirit of Hitler to guide him...

Despite the intriguingly dark premise, He's Alive is a disappointing episode that even manages to waste the talents of Dennis Hopper. It's difficult to take him too seriously when Vollmer is preaching on street corners and we never truly believe he might attract any sort of following. The friendship between Vollmer and his father figure, a concentration camp survivor named Ernst (Ludwig Donath), feels unbelievable and even borderline tasteless and all in all Rod Serling did much better with these serious and harrowing themes in Deaths Head Revisited.

Deaths Head Revisited was more haunting and chilling in exploring the tragic and dangerous power that extreme ideologies can hold over individuals. He's Alive is encapsulated in the moment when Curt Conway as the mysterious mentor steps out of the shadows and reveals he is Hitler. He looks like someone at a fancy dress party who barely resembles Hitler. The main problem with He's Alive is that it's a rather boring and uninteresting experience as a piece of entertainment. The fact that it runs for an hour instead of half an hour makes it feel even worse. This is definitely one of those hour long Twilight Zones where you may end up checking your watch and wondering how much more of this you have to sit through.

He's Alive is a strangely dull episode given the premise and subject matter. The intention here was presumably to expose the banality and immorality of those that follow extreme such ideologies but despite the worthy intentions this episode ends up feeling oddly pointless and flat. This is arguably the worst episode in season four and never really works despite what seems on the face of it a mildly intriguing premise. C-

MUTE (Director: Stuart Rosenberg, Writer: Richard Matheson)

"What you're witnessing is the curtain-raiser to a most extraordinary play; to wit, the signing of a pact, the commencement of a project. The play itself will be performed almost entirely offstage. The final scenes are to be enacted a decade hence and with a different cast. The main character of these final scenes is Ilse, the daughter of Professor and Mrs Nielsen, age two. At the moment she lies sleeping in her crib, unaware of the singular drama in which she is to be involved. Ten years from this moment, Ilse Nielsen is to know the desolating terror of living simultaneously in the world and in the Twilight Zone."

A group of people in Germany in the fifties form a community that has developed telepathic powers and have children that do not speak. A family from the community moves to the United States but both parents are killed in a house fire. Their last act is to use their mental powers to warn and save their young telepathic mute daughter Ilse (Ann Jillian). The orphaned Ilse is taken in by Sheriff Harry Wheeler (Robert Boon) and his wife Cora (Barbara Baxley) while they try to locate any relatives she might have. Not understanding the true nature of Ilse, the pair are appalled that she doesn't seem to be able to speak or read and enroll her in a school where a strict, insensitive and sadistic teacher named Edna Frank (Irene Dailey) becomes determined to make Ilse just like everyone else.

While Sheriff Wheeler tries to make contact with any family the mute orphan might have in Germany, he is unaware that his wife is burning the letters and doing everything she can to make sure that Ilse never leaves. Their own daughter drowned in an accident and Cora is maniacally determined to maintain possession of Ilse - who she is irrationally believes is her own daughter somehow returned to her. In the middle of all of this is Ilse, marooned, alone and isolated in her own mind, and unable to communicate with anyone...

Mute is an interesting episode that is well crafted and well performed but one that is also - it has to be said - maybe just a little dull too at times, especially with the longer running time of season four. This is another story that would probably have a better reputation if it was only half an hour long. Child actress Ann Jillian is excellent in the central part of Ilse and although she can only use facial expressions and voiceovers she brings a depth and empathy to the part. We get a sense of how adrift she is in a world where everyone speaks and she is mute and telepathic. Voices are booming and scary to her and her own speech is just a garble.

Irene Dailey certainly brings gusto to her part as the teacher who has it in for Ilse. "We're going to work with her until she's exactly like everyone else!" Mute is rather dark with Ilse imprisoned in a world she can't communicate with and that can't possibly understand her.

Mute's end message is a trifle confusing because it seems to advocate conformity (most Twilight Zone stories are naturally against conformity!) but maybe that perception is misplaced or lost in translation. Ultimately, Mute is an interesting but not terribly exciting episode. It's not really something that will stay with you for very long or lodge in the memory much.

By the way, look for an appearance by Twilight Zone regular Oscar Beregi Jr. Mute doesn't exactly sound like a barrel of laughs and for good reason: it isn't. Aside from Ilse, none of the characters are very sympathetic, even the Sheriff and his wife (who comes across as somewhat hysterical and weird although I'm not even sure this was supposed to be the intention as she is clearly meant to be the nicest person here). B-

DEATH SHIP (Director: Don Medford, Writer: Richard Matheson)

"Picture of the spaceship E-89, cruising above the thirteenth planet of star system fifty-one, the year 1997. In a little while, supposedly, the ship will be landed and specimens taken: vegetable, mineral and, if any, animal. These will be brought back to overpopulated Earth, where technicians will evaluate them and, if everything is satisfactory, stamp their findings with the word 'inhabitable' and open up yet another planet for colonization. These are the things that are supposed to happen. Picture of the crew of the spaceship E-89: Captain Ross, Lieutenant Mason, Lieutenant Carter. Three men who have just reached a place which is as far from home as they will ever be. Three men who in a matter of minutes will be plunged into the darkest nightmare reaches of the Twilight Zone."

The three man crew of a spaceship land on a planet looking for scientific samples to return back to Earth. But what they find is shocking indeed. An exact replica of their ship containing their dead bodies!

A really good episode, Death Ship is great spooky fun with the very fifties pulp sci-fi spaceship designs and a wonderful mystery that taxes the crew to their limit. In many ways Death Ship is like one of the best episodes of Star Trek never made. The story is genuinely creepy when the characters make their alarming discovery and their attempts to make sense of this strange situation are nicely explored by the screenplay. The expanded nature of series four's episodes have already proved to be a problem but Death Ship actually benefits from having more time to develop its atmosphere and puzzle.

The icing on the cake is the presence of Twilight Zone legend Jack Klugman as Captain Ross and there's able support from the excellent Ross Martin (here making his second trip to The Twilight Zone). You generally KNOW that a Twilight Zone episode is going to be good if Jack Klugman is in it. Death Ship is a fun mystery - although it was probably a lot more original when Matheson conceived it. I've lost count of how many science fiction doppelganger/are we or are we not dead? capers there have been since. The crew start to think they are indeed dead but the stubborn Captain Ross won't hear a word of it. Death Ship becomes rather dreamlike at times and there's a touching scene involving Ross Martin's character and his child. Death Ship is not perfect but it is very good and the retro sci-fi trappings are a lot of fun. B+

JESS-BELLE (Director: Buzz Kulik, Writer: Earl Hamner Jr)

"The Twilight Zone has existed in many lands in many times. It has its roots in history, in something that happened long, long ago and got told about and handed down from one generation of folk to the other. In the telling the story gets added to and embroidered on, so that what might have happened in the time of the Druids is told as if it took place yesterday in the Blue Ridge Mountains. Such stories are best told by an elderly grandfather on a cold winter's night by the fireside in the southern hills of the Twilight Zone."

Jilted and jealous country girl Jess-Belle Stone (Anne Francis) makes a pact with a witch named Granny Hart (Jeanette Nolan) to win back old love Billy-Ben Turner (James Best). Billy-Ben has proposed to Ellwyn Glover (Laura Devon) but Jess-Belle is determined to put a stop to the wedding...

This is a pretty good episode from Waltons creator Earl Hamner Jr and Jess-Belle has a superb off-kilter country atmosphere where magic and darkness might well conceivably take flight when the moon rises. What really elevates the episode though is the superb casting. Anne Francis returns to the series in a very different part from The After Hours, her blonde hair now black and long. She's superb as the scheming, naive and tragic Jess-Belle. James Best also returns and has believable chemistry with Francis while Jeanette Nolan is memorable is her scenes as the witch Granny Hart.

Jess-Bell is sort of like The Waltons, Bewitched, Cat People and Faust all blended together and the end result is certainly engaging and enjoyable. There is a remarkably clever layer of double meaning in the script which is all the more remarkable for the fact that Hamner Jr apparently wrote his draft in a few days because they needed a story to film as quickly as possible. Even so, in the hands of the wrong cast Jess-Belle could easily have been dull and rather tiresome in the longer format but the cast is a delight. Though love potions and witchcraft are hardly original plot devices in an anthology show these elements are made fun here and this episode is generally very watchable. You wouldn't say that Jess-Belle is a classic but it is an agreeable and solid episode in season four.

The chemistry between Francis and Best as actors makes it easy to accept that the characters had a past together. Jeanette Nolan though probably steals the show as Granny Hart. When we first see her she is cloaked and hovering over a bubbling pot like your stereotypical witch. When Jess-Belle knocks on the door she suddenly seems to change as if by magic into a more presentable figure but her true nature is never too far way. "Why child, there ain't much I don't know," she tells Jess-Belle and we KNOW that the title character is unwisely meddling with things she doesn't understand all because she wants someone to love. This is a more whimsical episode but a good one and certainly one of the best acted and produced stories in this season. B

MINIATURE (Director: Walter Grauman, Writer: Charles Beaumont)

"To the average person, a museum is a place of knowledge, a place of beauty and truth and wonder. Some people come to study, others to contemplate, others to look for the sheer joy of looking. Charley Parkes has his own reasons. He comes to the museum to get away from the world. It isn't really the sixty-cent cafeteria meal that has drawn him here every day, it's the fact that here in these strange, cool halls he can be alone for a little while, really and truly alone. Anyway, that's how it was before he got lost and wandered into... the Twilight Zone."

Charley Parkes (Robert Duvall) is a shy office worker who still lives with his mother. When he visits the museum during his lunch hour he falls in love with a little wooden doll (Claire Griswold) contained in a wonderful nineteenth century dollhouse...

Miniature is a beautiful and highly unusual love story and one of the best stories that Charles Beaumont ever wrote for the Twilight Zone. The episode is wonderfully made too. Each time Charley visits the museum he witnesses an elegant pantomime as the woman in the dollhouse is served tea by her maid and then visited by a male suitor who may not have the most noble intentions (Charley of course is most disturbed by this latter development). A full size replica of the dollhouse was constructed so that Claire Griswold could act these scenes and the care and expense that went into Miniature always shines through.

Key to it all is the fantastic performance by Robert Duvall as Charley, an intelligent and decent man who just can't face reality. He is not comfortable in his own skin nor with other human beings. Duvall gives a wonderfully understated performance that is both moving and believable. Great scene where Charley is sent on a blind date by his sister with a more worldly woman named Harriet (Joan Chambers). It ends in disaster when Harriet makes a pass at Charley and the terrified bachelor has no idea what to do, his frozen unresponsive hesitancy interpreted as a snub by the furious woman. Miniature comfortably maintains its gentle and delightfully strange spell over the course of its 60 or so minutes and has a fittingly touching and offbeat ending that doesn't disappoint.

A great episode. The synopsis might make Miniature sound silly but this is truly one of the most moving Twilight Zone stories and one where we really feel for the central character and want him to be ok. There's no doubt that this is a classic Twilight Zone episode and highly recommended. A

PRINTER'S DEVIL (Director: Ralph Senensky, Writer: Charles Beaumont)

"Take away a man's dream, fill him with whiskey and despair, send him to a lonely bridge, let him stand there all by himself looking down at the black water, and try to imagine the thoughts that are in his mind. You can't, I can't. But there's someone who can, and that someone is seated next to Douglas Winter right now. The car is headed back toward town, but its real destination is the Twilight Zone."

Struggling small town newspaper editor Douglas Winter (Robert Sterling) is saved from suicide by the mysterious Mr Smith (Burgess Meredith). Not only that but Smith also saves his ailing newspaper. But how does Smith get the journalistic scoops on all the horrible disasters that seem to happen?

Though somewhat obvious at times, Printer's Devil is an entertaining entry in series four with the fun vintage newspaper office/printing scenes and Burgess Meredith enjoying himself as the thoroughly diabolical Mr Smith. Perhaps the most memorable scene occurs when Smith teases Winter about signing his eternal soul over to him while simultaneously declaring it a ludicrous concept. Is it a ludicrous concept? Not in the Twilight Zone that's for sure.

The last act wraps everything up a trifle too easily in the end but Printer's Devil is certainly an entertaining ride along the way. Burgess Meredith particularly enjoyed playing Smith because the role was a departure from his usual put upon little man and enabled him to be fiendish, clever and wicked for a change. Mr Smith seems too good to be true in the manner in which he talks Winter out of suicide and then saves the newspaper and he is. What is nice here is the way that Smith seems like an eccentric old man who is trying to do the paper a favour but gradually ends up taking more and more control, especially as he is the only person who can make head nor tail of the strange old fashioned printing presses he has set up, these machines spookily able to predict the future.

The two leads here are well served by Beaumont's dialogue in what becomes a battle of wits between them. The relationship between Winter and Smith gradually shifts over the course of the story until Smith seems to be holding all the cards. Has Winter left it too late by not realising just how dangerous this little old man is? The cost will be far greater than his newspaper if he doesn't come up with a solution. Printer's Devil's is good stuff on the whole and - happily - breezes past in entertaining fashion and doesn't feel overlong at all despite having an hour to fill. The Twilight Zone had explored such themes many times before in a whimsical fashion but there is an underlying menace to Printer's Devil that always give the story a big boost. B+

NO TIME LIKE THE PAST (Director: Justus Addiss, Writer: Rod Serling)

"Exit one Paul Driscoll, a creature of the twentieth century. He puts to a test a complicated theorem of space-time continuum, but he goes a step further, or tries to. Shortly, he will seek out three moments of the past in a desperate attempt to alter the present, one of the odd and fanciful functions in a shadowland known as the Twilight Zone."

A scientist named Paul Driscoll (Dana Andrews) is unhappy with the modern world and seeks to make it a better place by altering key moments in time - specifically Hiroshima, Adolf Hitler and the Lusitania. Driscoll will discover though that altering the past is not as simple as it appears in theory...

Yet another time travel episode but not one of the best examples of this frequent anthology subgenre. The extended length really makes this story feel padded and Serling's script is uncharacteristically lazy and riddled with plot holes that merely perplex the viewer. Driscoll's key points in time are things like the rise of Hitler and Hiroshima but his approach to tackling these dark events do not seem to feature much logic. He arrives at Hiroshima with precious little time to spare before the attack so why bother at all? Serling admitted at the time that time travel had probably been done to death in The Twilight Zone by now and No Time Like the Past is certainly evidence of that.

This story also reminds you somewhat of an earlier Twilight Zone episode called Back There - which was equally forgettable. All in all, No Time Like the Past is a disappointing episode. The best scene in the whole episode actually comes when Driscoll lands in 1881 and ends up debating military policy with a gung-ho hotel guest. This is a brief moment of inspiration from Serling. Dana Andrews is passable in the lead but this is a story that really struggles with the longer format and begins to drag long before it reaches the end. No Time Like the Past is pretty uninspired on the whole and feels rather like yet another pale rehash of The Time Element. C+

THE PARALLEL (Director: Alan Crosland, Writer: Rod Serling)

"In the vernacular of space, this is T minus one hour. Sixty minutes before a human being named Major Robert Gaines is lifted off from the Mother Earth and rocketed into the sky, farther and longer than any man ahead of him. Call this one of the first faltering steps of man to sever the umbilical cord of gravity and stretch out a fingertip toward an unknown. Shortly, we'll join this astronaut named Gaines and embark on an adventure, because the environs overhead - the stars, the sky, the infinite space - are all part of a vast question mark known as the Twilight Zone."

When astronaut Major Robert Gaines (Steve Forrest) returns from a space mission his wife Helen (Jacqueline Scott) and daughter Maggie (Shari Bernath) soon begin to suspect he is not the person they remember...

The Parallel is a fairly bog standard alternate reality episode that is competent and mildly interesting at times but ultimately flat and dull and sunk by the longer running time as much as anything. The episode is rather predictable in the end and once the story returns to Earth the episode becomes rather bland. With more energy it might have made a decent thirty minute episode but the premise is stretched out for far too long and becomes tiresome in the end. There is no great twist here as the title of the episode gives away what is fairly obvious to us about ten minutes in anyway.

They had actually intended for Mr and Mrs Gaines to become aware there was something slightly different about each other after they went to bed for the first time since his return from space but to even hint at this was ultimately considered too risque in the censorship climate of the era.

The Parallel definitely has a tired going through the motions feel as if everyone knew this wasn't the greatest (or most original) script in the world and that it wasn't going to be a classic.

It's a very bog standard sort of episode that probably would have been forgettable over thirty minutes let alone padded out to an hour. This is pretty dull stuff in the end despite the early intrigue. C+

I DREAM OF GENIE (Director: Robert Gist, Writer: John Furia Jr)

"Meet Mr George P Hanley, a man life treats without deference, honor or success. Waiters serve his soup cold. Elevator operators close doors in his face. Mothers never bother to wait up for the daughters he dates. George is a creature of humble habits and tame dreams. He's an ordinary man, Mr Hanley, but at this moment the accidental possessor of a very special gift, the kind of gift that measures men against their dreams, the kind of gift most of us might ask for first and possibly regret to the last, if we, like Mr George P Hanley, were about to plunge head-first and unaware into our own personal Twilight Zone."

George Hanley (Howard Morris) is a sappy nobody. After deciding to buy a birthday present for Anne (Patricia Barry), the sexy secretary who works in the same office, he buys an old Arabian lamp for $20. When another office worker, the smug and handsome Roger (Mark Miller), gives Anne a revealing negligee George becomes too embarrassed to offer his present and takes the lamp home. You can probably guess where this is going. After polishing the lamp a very modern genie (Jack Albertson) appears and grants him one wish. As he only has one wish George has to think very carefully about this and we are presented with a series of scenarios that he daydreams as he ponders this difficult question. Should he wish for love? For money? Power? Each of the scenarios feature Anne and Roger in various guises. What will George wish for in the end?

Faust meets the old Genie caper in this treading water episode that plays like a dated sitcom. It should be more fun to encroach on George's fantasy situations but I Dream of Genie never really engages and would have been better off played over twenty-five minutes or so rather than be part of the extended season four stories. The four different tableaux are mildly diverting but seem rather loosely strung together (the ending feels like a desperate attempt to give a vague and rambling episode a twist) and the script is never terribly inventive or amusing.

For an episode like this to work you probably need more charm and a shorter running time. Also, the genie at the start tells George not to wish for wealth or love because neither of those wishes work so it doesn't make much sense anyway. Howard Morris is ok in the lead role but I Dream of Genie is not an episode you will feel a great yearning to return to much if at all. This sort of premise was done much better in the Peter Cook/Dudley Moore film Bedazzled. C+

THE NEW EXHIBIT (Director: John Brahm, Writer: Charles Beaumont and Jerry Sohl)

"Martin Lombard Senescu, a gentle man, the dedicated curator of murderers' row in Ferguson's Wax Museum. He ponders the reasons why ordinary men are driven to commit mass murder. What Mr Senescu does not know is that the groundwork has already been laid for his own special kind of madness and torment found only in the Twilight Zone."

Martin Senescu (Martin Balsam) inherits some wax figures of famous historical murderers when the museum he works in closes down. But the figures soon seem to exert a strange control over Martin...

After three dull episodes in a row, season four gets back on track with a fun horror episode that might be somewhat lax in the logic department but is very entertaining anyway with the wonderfully eerie wax figures and Balsam as the increasingly frazzled and unhinged Martin Senescu attempting to look after them and conceal an escalating body count. The New Exhibit doesn't seem to have a tremendously high reputation but I've always had fun with this episode and find it to be very enjoyable and entertaining. The wax figures (Jack the Ripper,

Albert W Hicks, Henri "Bluebeard" Landru, Hare and Burke)
and rather creepy and Martin Balsam is really good as a
Norman Bates type of character - which is fitting I suppose
because Balsam was actually in Psycho.

I like The New Exhibit because it's sort of tongue-in-cheek but
still quite straight and sinister. That sounds like a
contradiction but the tone is consistent and the episode strikes
the right balance between winking at the audience and telling
a little horror themed story. Martin's love for the figures is
probably the creepiest thing of all and his increasingly
desperate efforts to protect them supply the drama and give
the story impetus and a certain amount of intrigue. You
actually have sympathy for Senescu because he's lost his job
due to the museum being demolished to make way for a
supermarket. Senescu is naturally and rightly appalled by this
decision.

Martin begs to be allowed to save the five figures and take
them home with him so that they can be used if he fulfils his
dream of opening his own museum. He is granted this request
although his wife Emma (Maggie Mahoney) isn't too thrilled to
have these creepy artifacts in their basement where the air
conditioning electricity bill to keep them cool is soon
bankrupting them. Emma confides in her brother Dave
(William Mims) and he suggests she secretly disconnect the air
conditioner. However, these famous killers from the past do
not take kindly to this or any intervention at all and the body
count at the Senescu house soon begins to pile up.

The ending of this episode rather contradicts itself but I don't
think it really matters. This is a comic horror episode of The
Twilight Zone - not Ingmar Bergman. Who cares?

The New Exhibit is strong on atmosphere and has a
predictable but very enjoyable coda to neatly wrap things up.
This is a fun horror episode. B+

OF LATE I THINK OF CLIFFORDVILLE (Director: David Lowell Rich, Writer: Rod Serling)

"Witness a murder. The killer is Mr. William Feathersmith, a robber baron whose body composition is made up of a refrigeration plant covered by thick skin. In a moment Mr. Feathersmith will proceed on his daily course of conquest and calumny with yet another business dealing. But this one will be one of those bizarre transactions that take place in an odd marketplace known as the Twilight Zone."

A ruthless and arrogant veteran business tycoon named Bill Feathersmith (Albert Salmi) is given a chance to return to 1910 as a young man to make his fortune all over again but it doesn't prove to be quite as easy as he remembered...

Another time travel story, Of Late I Think of Cliffordville is a so-so episode that is worth the effort for Twilight Zone regular Albert Salmi (always great value although the old age makeup he is saddled with at the start could have been more convincing) and Julie Newmar (who played Catwoman in the Adam West Batman series) as the Devilish Miss Delin. The story itself is always quite interesting with a decent sense of period detail when Feathersmith returns to his dim and distant past. John Anderson is good here as Diedrich - a businessman who Feathersmith humiliates and swindles at the start of the story.

Though the logic in this story is not exactly what you would describe as airtight the episode is interesting enough to mostly hold your attention although it does begin to creak and groan in places under the stress of having to expand itself to an hour. This is another of those season four episodes that probably would have been much better in a half hour format. Though far from perfect or a classic, Of Late I Think of Cliffordville is at least quite watchable and the premise of a bombastic businessman wanting to go back in time and start his empire from scratch simply to prove that he CAN is interesting and fairly decent fodder for a fantasy story. Of Late I Think of Cliffordville is nothing great but a decent enough episode. B-

THE INCREDIBLE WORLD OF HORACE FORD (Director: Abner Biberman, Writer: Reginald Rose)

"Mr Horace Ford, who has a preoccupation with another time, a time of childhood, a time of growing up, a time of street games, stickball and hide-'n-go-seek. He has a reluctance to check out a mirror and see the nature of his image: proof positive that the time he dwells in has already passed him by. But in a moment or two he'll discover that mechanical toys and memories and daydreaming and wishful thinking and all manner of odd and special events can lead one into a special province, uncharted and unmapped, a country of both shadow and substance known as the Twilight Zone."

Horace Ford (Pat Hingle) is a middle-aged toy designer who has never grown up and still behaves like a child at times. He is obsessed with the golden memories of his childhood but a visit to the Twilight Zone may teach him that those childhood memories were not so golden as he remembers...

A common Twilight Zone theme is the yearning to go home again, to escape back into the past and the apparently carefree days of childhood. The Incredible World of Horace Ford is almost like a companion piece to Walking Distance although not nearly as strong. It's still worth the effort though for the enjoyably old fashioned studio street sets and Pat Hingle's committed performance as Horace. The moral of this story is that you can't go home again and should live in the present rather than the past and The Incredible World of Horace Ford is always an interesting meditation on this well trodden theme.

The other theme of the story is selective memory. Horace

remembers his childhood as an idyllic time and yearns to go back there but he'll realise that it wasn't quite as perfect as he remembers. His mind has filtered out the bad things that happened and left him with ridiculously romantic and cherry picked memories. The Incredible World of Horace Ford is on the whole well made and acted and has interesting themes at its core. The main problem is the extended running time. One can't help thinking they could have easily told this story in half an hour. Having to pad out an entire hur unavoidably means that The Incredible World of Horace Ford begins to somewhat outstay its welcome at some point or other. B-

ON THURSDAY WE LEAVE FOR HOME (Director: Buzz Kulik, Writer: Rod Serling)

"This is William Benteen, who officiates on a disintegrating outpost in space. The people are a remnant society who left the Earth looking for a Millennium, a place without war, without jeopardy, without fear, and what they found was a lonely, barren place whose only industry was survival. And this is what they've done for three decades: survive; until the memory of the Earth they came from has become an indistinct and shadowed recollection of another time and another place. One month ago a signal from Earth announced that a ship would be coming to pick them up and take them home. In just a moment we'll hear more of that ship, more of that home, and what it takes out of mind and body to reach it. This is the Twilight Zone."

A small colony of human space explorers have been stranded on a desolate heat baked planet with two suns for thirty years. They are down to 187 survivors and that is mostly due to the energetic and enthusiastic leadership of the self-appointed "Captain" Benteen (James Whitmore). Benteen has maintained order and kept them going by telling stories about the wonder and beauty of Earth and how they'll all return one day. A rescue ship finally arrives under the command of Commander Sloane (Tim O'Connor). The colonists are saved at last and begin the preparations for when the meteor storm will allow the ship to safely take off again. But as the colonists prepare to evacuate and go home, Benteen starts to mentally unravel at the thought of no longer being in charge of them...

This is easily Rod Serling's best contribution to series four and one of the best Twilight Zone stories he ever wrote. On Thursday We Leave for Home works on every level. It looks expensive, the acting is superb and the dialogue is great. James Whitmore's Captain Benteen is an unforgettable creation. At the start we suspect he might be a great man and his organisation, energy, and poetic tales of Earth while they take refuge in caves during meteor showers keep everyone going. Once the rescue ship arrives and Benteen loses his authority to Commander Sloane, he becomes petty, bitter, angry, jealous and altogether too human. From god to tyrant.

It's a great performance by Whitmore and Serling's dialogue is enjoyably purple at times. Some of the best scenes involve Benteen huddling with the others in a huge cave during meteor storms and telling the children about Earth. "I remember it as... a place of colour. I remember that in the autumn the leaves changed, turned different colours - red, orange, gold. I remember streams of water that flowed down hillsides, and the water was sparkling and clear. I remember the clouds in the sky, white, billowy things, floated like ships, like sails, and I remember night skies. Night skies. Like endless black velvet, with stars, sometimes a moon - hung as if suspended by wires, lit from inside..."

Benteen turns on the very people he's devoted the last thirty years of his life to protecting because he can't face the thought of them not needing him anymore. Benteen can't bear the thought of losing his authority and suggests they should all live together on Earth under his leadership. When discontent is grumbled at that suggestion he begins to become more and more embittered. He begins telling them Earth is actually a terrible place and even considers sabotage. On Thursday We Leave for Home is a brilliant story about ego and the dangers of becoming addicted to power. This is a well directed episode too with the craggy planet surface sets and the huge caves. On Thursday We Leave for Home is great stuff. A

PASSAGE ON THE LADY ANNE (Director: Lamont Johnson, Writer: Charles Beaumont)

"Portrait of a honeymoon couple getting ready for a journey - with a difference. These newlyweds have been married for six years, and they're not taking this honeymoon to start their life but rather to save it, or so Eileen Ransome thinks. She doesn't know why she insisted on a ship for this voyage, except that it would give them some time and she'd never been on one before - certainly never one like the Lady Anne. The tickets read 'New York to Southampton,' but this old liner is going somewhere else. Its destination - the Twilight Zone."

Businessman Allan Ransome (Lee Phillips) and his wife Ellen (Joyce Van Patten) travel to England by ship rather than plane because she wants time to repair their marriage. Their ship -The Lady Anne - is slow, charts an erratic course, and seems to be populated entirely by very old people. An elderly couple named McKenzie (Wilfred Hyde-White) and Millie (Gladys Copper) attempt to persuade them not to travel on the ship and even offer $10,000 for their tickets. Annoyed at this, Allan brushes off the offer. What is the secret of the Lady Anne?

Passage on the Lady Anne is more of a gentle, sweet episode but dreadfully slow and talky. There is no major twist (the ending is rather cryptic) and it's really about a couple trying to save their marriage in unusual circumstances. This really only of interest for the presence of many veteran British actors who are all very polished and charming and make the episode modestly watchable if nothing else. Look out for Alan Napier (Alfred the butler in the Adam West Batman television series).

This is a strange episode that never feels much like a Twilight Zone story. It's certainly pleasant enough and the cast is good (Gladys Cooper returns and seems to be enjoying herself) but it is ultimately not the most exciting or intriguing Twilight Zone story and rather dull in the end. This is also yet another episode in season four that is rather hobbled by the extended running time of this season. You really didn't need an hour of this - and it just makes the episode feel even slower than it already is. Passage on the Lady Anne could have, with some changes and edits, been an acceptable half hour episode but the romance and whimsy on offer here is spread way too thin for an hour long show. C+

THE BARD (Director: Herbert Hirschman, Writer: Rod Serling)

"You've just witnessed opportunity, if not knocking, at least scratching plaintively on a closed door. Mr Julius Moomer, a would-be writer who, if talent came twenty-five cents a pound, would be worth less than car fare. But, in a moment, Mr Moomer, through the offices of some black magic, is about to embark on a brand-new career. And although he may never get a writing credit on the Twilight Zone, he's to become an integral character in it."

Struggling writer Julius Moomer (Jack Weston) is full of ideas but has no talent. His agent Gerald (Henry Lasco) is so desperate to get Julius out of this office he asks him to write a pilot for a black magic series and says he'll submit it if he writes it by Monday. Julius buys a book about black magic for research and ends up summoning the spirit of Shakespeare (John Williams) - who he enlists as his ghost writer...

The Bard is a passable comic episode in which Rod Serling is clearly enjoying having a few digs at the television and the writing industry. This is probably one of the best of Serling's more comic slanted scripts. It's all amusing enough when Shakespeare complains about the changes being made to his scripts and not receiving sufficient story credit.

The episode is helped too by the excellent performances of the well cast Weston and Williams. The Bard is clever and quite likeable but it is slight and - at the risk of repeating myself - anther season four entry that probably would have worked just as well if not even better in a half hour format.

The Bard passes the time and is agreeable enough but it never really threatens to be a classic despite its generally likeable and entertaining qualities. By the way, look out here for a young Burt Reynolds as a Brando type actor. There are some decent jokes and situations in The Bard and one has the impression that Rod Serling enjoyed writing this screenplay. This is a passable end to what has been - with a few notable exceptions - a middling sort of season. One would have to say that the hour long format didn't really suit The Twilight Zone for the most part. Too many of these stories felt dragged out beyond their material. Still, any season with classics like On Thursday We Leave for Home, Miniature, and Death Ship can't be construed as bad. B-

The Fifth Season 1963/1964

IN PRAISE OF PIP (Director: Joseph M Newman, Writer: Rod Serling)

"Submitted for your approval, one Max Phillips, a slightly the worse for wear maker of book, whose life has been as drab and undistinguished as a bundle of dirty clothes. And though it's very late in his day, he has an errant wish that the rest of his life might be sent out to a laundry to come back shiny and clean, this to be a gift of love to a son named Pip. Mr Max Phillips, Homo sapiens, who is soon to discover that man is not as wise as he thinks, said lesson to be learned in the Twilight Zone..."

An alcoholic bookie named Max Phillips (Jack Klugman) who has made something of a mess of his life. When he learns that his son Pip (played by Billy Mumy and Bobby Diamond respectively at different ages) has been critically wounded fighting in Vietnam, Max feels an overwhelming sense of guilt and remorse for not having been a better father. Determined to be a better person from now on, he returns $300 to a hopeless gambler and receives a bullet from one of the goons of his ruthless boss in return. Max staggers into an abandoned funfair at night where visions of his son begin to appear...

In Praise of Pip is a strong opener for the final season and - thankfully - the hour long episode structure has been abandoned and we are back to the shorter format. In Praise of Pip is deeply moving and features another knockout performance by Jack Klugman. This is a poignant and dreamlike episode that becomes very moving towards the end and the presence of Klugman stops it from ever sliding into bathos. It's a very moving story about a man's love for his son and yearning to turn back the clock and be a better person.

This episode was shot at Pacific Ocean Park in Santa Monica and the deserted theme park makes a suitably solemn and strange location for the story with the hall of mirrors in particular nicely used by the director when Max catches glimpses of the young Pip as he unsteadily and woozily makes his way around the funfair. This was actually the first American television episode of just about anything to ever mention the Vietnam conflict in relation to the human cost and casualties. "Pip is dying. My kid is dying. In a place called South Vietnam. There isn't even supposed to be a war going on there, but my son is dying. It's to laugh. I swear it's to laugh." In Praise of Pip is very strong all round and one of the more poignant Twilight Zone entries. It's one of the more grim Twilight Zone stories but worth the effort. B+

STEEL (Director: Don Weis, Writer: Richard Matheson)

"Sports item, circa 1974: Battling Maxo, B2, heavyweight, accompanied by his manager and handler, arrives in Maynard, Kansas, for a scheduled six-round bout. Battling Maxo is a robot, or, to be exact, an android, definition: 'an automaton resembling a human being.' Only these automatons have been permitted in the ring since prizefighting was legally abolished in 1968. This is the story of that scheduled six-round bout, more specifically the story of two men shortly to face that remorseless truth: that no law can be passed which will abolish cruelty or desperate need - nor, for that matter, blind animal courage. Location for the facing of said truth a small, smoke-filled arena just this side of the Twilight Zone."

In the near future the sport of boxing is banned for human participants but - because people still love to gamble on the fights - continues with human looking robots doing the fighting. When his robot boxer Battling Maxo (Tipp McClure) breaks down, boxing manager Steel Kelly (Marvin) decides to secretly take his place in the big fight to earn enough money for repairs - despite knowing he'll most likely take a fearful pounding in the process...

This is a strange but very watchable episode adapted from a 1956 short story Matheson wrote for The Magazine of Fantasy and Science Fiction. It was later reworked into a film vehicle for Hugh Jackman. The boxing match here is very well staged and the robots (played by human actors of course) are nicely done. Basically very stoic and mask like faces with deliberate movements.

It probably doesn't make an awful lot of sense for Steel Kelly to insist on going through with the fight when there must surely be other ways for them to get some money but maybe that's the whole point of the story. Steel is an uncomplicated character with an obstinate streak of stubbornness. The more he's pleaded with to not go through with the boxing deception the more he insists on doing it. The story always gets a boost from the presence of Lee Marvin as the incredibly stubborn Steel Kelly, a man who is willing to make heavy sacrifices simply to get by. The old fashioned downbeat treatment of this strange future sport works well throughout. Steel is definitely an odd episode and falls some way short of being a classic but it is very watchable. B-

NIGHTMARE AT 20,000 FEET (Director: Richard Donner, Writer: Richard Matheson)

"Portrait of a frightened man: Mr Robert Wilson, thirty-seven, husband, father, and salesman on sick leave. Mr Wilson has just been discharged from a sanatorium where he spent the last six months recovering from a nervous breakdown, the onset of which took place on an evening not dissimilar to this one, on an airliner very much like the one in which Mr Wilson is about to be flown home - the difference being that, on that evening half a year ago, Mr Wilson's flight was terminated by the onslaught of his mental breakdown. Tonight, he's travelling all the way to his appointed destination, which, contrary to Mr Wilson's plan, happens to be in the darkest corner of the Twilight Zone..."

Bob Wilson (William Shatner) suffered a complete nervous breakdown on a plane and was sent to an institution as a result. After six months though he was deemed fit enough to leave and is flying home. Wilson is apparently recovered - until that is he sees a strange creature out on the wing...

This is one of the most famous of all Twilight Zone episodes and was originally a short story called Alone in the Night. Nightmare at 20,000 Feet has a wonderfully simple premise and plays it well. As Bob settles into his seat, a storm begins to rattle the plane and buffet the passengers - hardly helping Wilson's mild apprehension about being in the air again. He peers out of the window through the arcs of rain and sparks of lightning and sees what appears to be the outline of a man on the wing. Closer inspection reveals the figure to be not a man but some type of strange furry gremlin creature intentionally damaging the plane! Is it real or a figment of Wilson's imagination?

Shatner's character works slightly better here than John Lithgow in the (very good and worth watching) 1983 Twilight Zone Movie remake of this for a specific reason that Richard Matheson was always quick to note himself. Shatner begins the story sane and calm and becomes increasingly unhinged whereas Lithgow seems to be at the end of his rope from the start! The general gist here is that Wilson keeps seeing the creature but when he alerts someone and they have a look it has peskily flown away. It naturally makes them all think he's gone completely mad and he starts to question his sanity himself.

There is a good deal of tension when Bob starts to feel he has to do something to save the plane - even though no one believes him. He hatches a scheme to steal a policeman's gun and this is an enjoyably and amusingly Shatner-esque acting masterclass! The creature is a bit risible now (just a man in a suit) but Nightmare at 20,000 Feet is still classic Twilight Zone. Nightmare at 20,000 Feet is one of the best ideas that anyone ever came up with for a Twilight Zone episode and a lot of fun. A

A KIND OF STOPWATCH (Director: John Rich, Writer: Michael D Rosenthal)

"Submitted for your approval or at least your analysis: one Patrick Thomas McNulty, who at age forty-one is the biggest bore on Earth. He holds a ten-year record for the most meaningless words spewed out during a coffee break. And it's very likely that, as of this moment, he would have gone through life in precisely this manner, a dull, argumentative bigmouth who sets back the art of conversation a thousand years. I say he very likely would have, except for something that will soon happen to him, something that will considerably alter his existence and ours. Now you think about that now, because this is the Twilight Zone."

Patrick McNulty (Richard Erdman) is one of the most boring men on the planet and never stops talking. After being fired from his job, he goes to a bar where he irritates everyone intensely with his propensity to jabber away and be very familiar whether they want to talk to him or not. However, when he buys a sozzled man named Potts (Leon Belasco) a drink, Potts gives him a watch as a gift. But this is no ordinary watch. If you click the button on the top it freezes time...

You'll see the twist coming a mile away and the plot is unavoidably contrived (if this watch is so special why does a drunk simply hand it over to McNutly?) but A Kind of Stopwatch is (ahem) watchable enough if a little on the broad side (this is another Serling script that veers towards comedy though in not so jarring a fashion as some of his more forgettable lighter Twilight Zones).

The premise here is sort of fun (frozen time capers were rather less hackneyed in the early sixties than they are these days I suppose) and the twist is decent even if you might see it coming but there is a definite slap dash aura to this episode that loses marks. Erdman is also a bit too frantic and eager in the lead role. McNulty decides he will use this incredible device to rob a bank in the story but this being The Twilight Zone will inevitably get more than he bargained for meddling with frozen time shenanigans. A Kind of Stopwatch, despite its comic ambience, does manage to generate some atmosphere and dread when we reach the coda. This episode is no classic but it's mildly entertaining and not bad at all. There is nice irony to the McGuffin. The watch is the ultimate conversation piece but as it freezes time and all those around McNulty it stops conversation stone dead too! B-

THE LAST NIGHT OF A JOCKEY (Director: Joseph M Newman, Writer: Rod Serling)

"The name is Grady, five-feet short in stockings and boots, a slightly distorted offshoot of a good breed of humans who race horses. He happens to be one of the rotten apples, bruised and yellowed by dealing in dirt, a short man with a short memory who's forgotten that he's worked for the sport of kings and helped turn it into a cesspool, used and misused by the two-legged animals who've hung around sporting events since the days of the Coliseum. So this is Grady, on his last night as a jockey. Behind him are Hialeah, Hollywood Park and Saratoga. Rounding the far turn and coming up fast on the rail is the Twilight Zone."

Grady (Mickey Rooney) is a jockey who was banned from the track for horse doping. He now sits alone in his ramshackle room contemplating the apparent end of his career and the mess he's made of his life. Grady engages in an overwrought dialogue with his conscience or a sort of Twilight Zone higher power and asks to be granted a wish. As ever though in the Twilight Zone he should be careful what he wishes for...

Written as a showcase for Mickey Rooney, The Last Night of a Jockey is like an inferior version of Nervous Man in a Four Dollar Room and Rooney's scenery chewing soon starts to grate in what is a very dull and strange episode. The twist is telegraphed and we never care an awful lot about his character to make his fate of huge importance. This is definitely one of those final season episodes that feels like the last scrapings from the bottom of the barrel. Neither the character nor the scenario are interesting enough to hook us or hold our attention (who cares about a disgraced jockey?) and Rod Serling doesn't feel tremendously enthused himself if his script is anything to go by.

The Last Night of a Jockey begins to irritate and sag long before we reach the (groan) finish line and ends up as a fairly pointless and tedious sort of story. Mickey Rooney could be great with the right material but sadly he's not terribly well served here in this very forgettable Twilight Zone. You'd be better off watching Rooney's performance in Night Gallery several years later because at least he got to be in a much more entertaining story in that. D

LIVING DOLL (Director: Richard C Sarafian, Writer: Charles Beaumont and Jerry Sohl)

"Talky Tina, a doll that does everything, a lifelike creation of plastic and springs and painted smile. To Erich Streator, she is a most unwelcome addition to his household, but without her he'd never enter the Twilight Zone."

Annabelle Streator (Mary LaRoche) buys an expensive talking doll for her daughter Christie (Tracy Stratford) named "Talky Tina". But Christie's miserable stepfather Erich Streator (Telly Savalas) isn't too pleased and claims the last thing she needs is more dolls.

This attitude becomes even more pronounced when the doll starts making threats to him when they are alone! "My name is Talky Tina and I'm beginning to hate you!" Talky Tina soon makes it clear she is going to get rid of Erich but he can't tell anyone or they'll think he's gone mad. He decides he will secretly destroy the doll but this proves to be much easier said than done...

Living Doll is a fun horror episode to perk up the sometimes patchy series five. If you can't enjoy Telly Savalas being persecuted by a toy doll then there is probably no hope for you. Savalas is well cast as the grumpy Erich and the doll is pretty creepy too and appropriately indestructible when the battle of will begins.

This is hardly the most original of premises to work from but Living Doll is good fun as far as it goes. This is a nice little chiller with spooky music by Bernard Herrman.

The premise is rather like one of the segments in those old Amicus horror anthologies and great fun. Inanimate objects who seem to have a secret life of their own was nothing new at the time - even to The Twilight Zone - but this is certainly one of the most enjoyable examples. I quite like the way we can read the story in more than one way. Talky Tina could be alive and protecting Christie from her wicked stepfather or Erich could simply be mad and hallucinating the whole thing.

The child actress Tracy Stratford is very good too and had already made her mark in the Twilight Zone with the Richard Matheson episode Little Girl Lost. B

THE OLD MAN IN THE CAVE
(Director: Alan Crosland Jr, Writer: Rod Serling)

"What you're looking at is a legacy that man left to himself. A decade previous he pushed his buttons and, a nightmarish moment later, woke up to find that he had set the clock back a thousand years. His engines, his medicines, his science were buried in a mass tomb, covered over by the biggest gravedigger of them all: a bomb. And this is the Earth ten years later, a fragment of what was once a whole, a remnant of what was once a race. The year is 1974, and this is the Twilight Zone."

A post-apocalyptic community somewhere in the United States has survived for ten years by following the instructions given to them by the "Old Man in the Cave" - who they've never actually seen for themselves. When Major French (James Coburn) and some soldiers arrive they pour scorn on this act of faith...

The Old Man in the Cave is a little slow moving but generally an interesting story about faith and man's reliance on technology. Twilight Zone staple John Anderson is well cast as Goldsmith, the man who tries to maintain the community's faith in the cave (most saliently the old man in the cave tells them what is safe to eat or drink and what is not) and his straight arrow character provides someone for Coburn's arrogant Major French to bounce off.

Major French assumes control and against the protests of Goldsmith begins handing out food and drink which the Old Man in the Cave claims is contaminated. French and his men believe that the people are idiots for listening to a mysterious old man who they have never even seen and soon decide they should all go to the cave and take a look for themselves. The revelation at the end raises some questions that the episode never completely answers but this is a good solid Twilight Zone story about faith and technology that gains a boost from the cast. The original Twilight Zone's wonderful black and white aura makes The Old Man in the Cave rather atmospheric too. This episode doesn't seem to have a glowingly high reputation but it's a pretty solid entry and makes for an absorbing enough half an hour of television. B

UNCLE SIMON (Director: Don Siegel, Writer: Rod Serling)

"Dramatis personae: Mr Simon Polk, a gentleman who has lived out his life in a gleeful rage; and the young lady who's just beat the hasty retreat is Mr Polk's niece, Barbara. She's lived her life as if during each ensuing hour she had a dentist appointment. There's yet a third member of the company soon to be seen. He now resides in the laboratory and he is the kind of character to be found only in the Twilight Zone."

Barbara (Constance Ford) loathes her old Uncle Simon (Cedric Hardwicke) and the feeling is mutual. She looks after him because she is the heir to his fortune but when he takes a tumble down the stairs she learns he's left a most unusual clause in his will and testament...

Uncle Simon is a bewildering black comedy episode that soon grows tiresome as Ford and Hardwicke hurl windy insults at one another. The episode crashes off a cliff altogether when the robot from Forbidden Planet turns up and Barbara has to wait on it as if it's a real person. Uncle Simon is one of those later Twilight Zone episodes that leaves you scratching your head somewhat and wondering why it was made.

The acid dripped insults the two characters hurl at each other are fun at first but quickly become grating (surely no one says what is on their mind like this in such a literal sense?) and the two characters are so completely unpleasant anyway you never really care what happens to them or if Barbara gets the money or not. By the time Robby the Robot is wheeled out you've just about given up with this one and are ready to move on. Uncle Simon is definitely not an episode to screen for anyone you are trying to introduce to The Twilight Zone. D

PROBE 7 - OVER AND OUT (Director: Ted Post, Writer: Rod Serling)

"One Colonel Cook, a traveler in space. He's landed on a remote planet several million miles from his point of departure. He can make an inventory of his plight by just one 360-degree movement of head and eyes. Colonel Cook has been set adrift in an ocean of space in a metal lifeboat that has been scorched and destroyed and will never fly again. He survived the crash but his ordeal is yet to begin. Now he must give battle to loneliness. Now Colonel Cook must meet the unknown. It's a small planet set deep in space. But for Colonel Cook, it's the Twilight Zone."

Colonel Cook (Richard Baseheart) crash-lands on a remote planet millions of miles away. When he receives a transmission from home telling him the that nuclear war is imminent on Earth he realises that there is no hope of a rescue mission and that he is now stranded. Exploring his new home, he soon realises he is not alone. Also stranded is Norda (Antoinette Bower), a space traveller and sole survivor from her home world. They must now try to understand each other and work out what to do on this new world...

Probe 7 - Over and Out is an average episode that never becomes anything special but is watchable enough with Richard Baseheart a good stock leading man and the transmissions of nuclear paranoia effective in establishing a sense of sorrow and atmosphere. Cook must explore what seems to be his new home and finds he isn't alone. There was potential here for an enjoyable Robinson Crusoe on Mars fashion caper but Probe 7 - Over and Out never quite lurches into life and the ending is rather predictable and so somewhat unsatisfying.

This goes as far as it does thanks to the actors and the mildly intriguing initial premise of Cook stranded millions of miles away from home with the knowledge that the world he knows is about to be destroyed. Probe 7 - Over and Out is a watchable episode but never much more than that. The initial premise here definitely leads one to expect a much better episode than we actually get but you wouldn't say this was a clunker by any means. Probe 7 - Over and Out is just very average in the end and not an episode you would say was either very good nor very bad. B-

THE 7th IS MADE UP OF PHANTOMS (Director: Alan Crosland Jr, Writer: Rod Serling)

"June 25th, 1964, or, if you prefer, June 25th, 1876. The cast of characters in order of their appearance: a patrol of General Custer's cavalry and a patrol of National Guardsmen on a manoeuvrer. Past and present are about to collide head-on, as they are wont to do in a very special bivouac area known as the Twilight Zone."

During National Guard training near Little Big Horn, a three man crew of a tank - William Connors (Ron Foster), Michael McCluskey (Randy Boone), Richard Langsford (Warren Oates) - hear what sounds like gunfire and then find a tepee and a canteen with the engraving "7th Cavalry". 7th Cavalry was the outfit led to their doom by General Custer in 1876. This is only the start of the strange occurrences for the men. They hear Indian war cries and see smoke signals. Somehow they seem to be in pursuit of the past and being dragged into this historical massacre. Should they intervene?

The 7th Is Made Up of Phantoms doesn't always make much sense but it is fun as far as it goes with the ghostly (and largely offscreen) Indian capers and increasing puzzlement of the tank crew. Extras are rather thin on the ground but then the focus on the tank crew makes the situation more tense and also of course makes the viewer use their imagination (a lost art in this CG festooned age). The three actors are rather dull to be honest and I would struggle to distinguish them even after watching the episode but this not bad at all.

One slight problem of course is the fact that the men presume Custer to have been on the side of good and have no qualms about throwing a tank into the battle to help him. A very romantic and one sided approach to this period of American history. The lack of any political commentary on the ethical logic of defending General Custer is noticeable by its absence. The 7th Is Made Up of Phantoms is no classic but it is watchable and always fairly interesting. This is not something though that is likely to land near the top of the pile when preparing for a Twilight Zone rewatch marathon. The 7th Is Made Up of Phantoms ultimately isn't that memorable at all. B-

A SHORT DRINK FROM A CERTAIN FOUNTAIN (Director: Bernard Girard, Writer: Rod Serling)

"Picture of an aging man who leads his life, as Thoreau said, 'in quiet desperation.' Because Harmon Gordon is enslaved by a love affair with a wife forty years his junior. Because of this, he runs when he should walk. He surrenders when simple pride dictates a stand. He pines away for the lost morning of his life when he should be enjoying the evening. In short, Mr Harmon Gordon seeks a fountain of youth, and who's to say he won't find it? This happens to be the Twilight Zone."

Harmon Gordon (Patrick O'Neal) is struggling to keep up with his forty years younger gold-digging wife Flora (Ruta Lee). Desperate to recapture his youth and please his wife (who thinks he is boring) he persuades his doctor brother Raymond (Walter Brooke) to inject him with an experimental youth serum. Will it work?

A Short Drink from a Certain Fountain is Rod Serling on autopilot but the cast give enough to just about make it worthwhile. This is a fairly slight but watchable episode that is a bit too wordy and predictable for its own good in the end but certainly not bad. Patrick O'Neal is fine as the put upon Gordon and I quite enjoyed Walter Brooke as his more sensible brother. Ruta Lee is ok as his glamorous and demanding (not to mention nasty) wife although you do wonder why Harmon would put up with her even if she is attractive!

The make-up effects are good here. O'Neal was only five years older than Ruta Lee in real life but made to look much older than her. The ending doesn't bear thinking about too much afterwards but it's a fair enough full circle coda for the episode at the conclusion. This episode was effectively blocked until the 1980s because of a dispute over the story. It's hard to believe that anyone could seriously claim to have invented such an old and well worn fantasy theme as the one deployed here! B-

NINETY YEARS WITHOUT SLUMBERING (Director: Roger Kay, Writer: "Richard DeRoy" - from a story by George Clayton Johnson)

"Each man measures his time; some with hope, some with joy, some with fear. But Sam Forstmann measures his allotted time by a grandfather's clock, a unique mechanism whose pendulum swings between life and death, a very special clock that keeps a special kind of time in the Twilight Zone."

Sam Forstmann (Ed Wynn) is knocking on for eighty years old and has an unshakable and irrational belief that when the grandfather clock he has owned all of his life stops ticking he will die too.

This obsession makes him a rather difficult person to live with as he is always paranoid about the clock and constantly checking on it. However, in order to placate his granddaughter Marnie (Carolyn Kearney) he agrees to sell the clock to a neighbour so long as he can visit and check on its maintenance on a regular basis. But when the neighbours go on holiday Sam soon becomes hysterical and fearful of the unattended clock winding down and attempts to break into their house...

Ninety Years Without Slumbering has an interesting premise but never quite manages to all come together and includes an ending that seems to go against the story we've been following.

George Clayton Johnson was so unhappy with the changes made to his story that he asked to have his name removed from the credits. This is a very average episode that goes as far as it does because of the warm and likeable of presence of Ed Wynn (in his second Twilight Zone story) and is a so so meditation on mortality and the passing of time.

Serling's narrations are probably the best thing here ("Clocks are made by men. God creates time. No man can prolong his allotted hours, he can only live them to the fullest - in this world or the Twilight Zone...")

This episode would probably be forgettable without Ed Wynn - who is charming as the eccentric but kind hearted old man. What helps this episode too is Sam's desperate attempt to get to his exiled grandfather clock before it can stop ticking. This adds a surprising dollop of tension to the story. B-

RING-A-DING GIRL (Director: Alan Crosland Jr, Writer: Earl Hamner Jr)

"Introduction to Bunny Blake. Occupation: film actress. Residence: Hollywood, California, or anywhere in the world that cameras happen to be grinding. Bunny Blake is a public figure; what she wears, eats, thinks, says is news. But underneath the glamour, the makeup, the publicity, the build-up, the costuming, is a flesh-and-blood person, a beautiful girl about to take a long and bizarre journey into the Twilight Zone."

Bunny Blake (Maggie McNamara) is a big film star on her way Rome by plane who receives a present from the Bunny Blake fan club in her home town of Howardville. Bunny looks into the ring and sees all the faces of the people she knew in Howardville and has an overwhelming feeling that she is needed there. She abandons her plans and returns home, dropping in on her surprised sister Hilday (Mary Munday) and nephew Bud (David Macklin). They are delighted to see their famous relative (for Bunny doesn't visit often). Bunny soon makes her presence felt around the town and when she learns that the Founder's Day picnic is on that day she organises a one-woman show at another part of town and tries to get everyone to attend that instead of the picnic. For what purpose?

This is one of the more underrated episodes of The Twilight Zone and very moving I think. Ring-a-Ding Girl takes a while to settle into but it is definitely worth your time.
Ring-a-Ding Girl seems a bit pat and dull at first but you gradually get into the episode and then all becomes clear at the end and you realise how it all fits together. The final shot of Maggie McNamara here is one of the single most moving and touching moments of any Twilight Zone episode and absolutely perfect.

Serling's final narration (which I won't repeat in this case for fear of spoilers) is superb too. Ring-a-Ding Girl probably won't be everyone's cup of tea and you might guess the ending before we actually get there but it's effective enough for what it is and a pretty decent Twilight Zone episode. B

YOU DRIVE (Director: John Brahm, Writer: Earl Hamner Jr)

"Portrait of a nervous man: Oliver Pope by name, office manager by profession. A man beset by life's problems: his job, his salary, the competition to get ahead. Obviously, Mr Pope's mind is not on his driving. Oliver Pope, businessman-turned-killer on a rain-soaked street in the early evening of just another day during just another drive home from the office. The victim, a kid on a bicycle, lying injured, near death. But Mr Pope hasn't time for the victim, his only concern is for himself. Oliver Pope, hit-and-run driver, just arrived at a crossroad in his life, and he's chosen the wrong turn. The hit occurred in the world he knows, but the run will lead him straight into the Twilight Zone."

Stressed office manager Oliver Pope (Edward Andrews) kills a paperboy in his car and drives away in panic. Pope decides to keep his guilt a secret but his spooky car has other ideas...

This is reminiscent of a much earlier Twilight Zone episode called A Thing About Machines but works better thanks in no small way to the sweaty and paranoid performance of Edward Andrews as the guilt stricken driver, a man who is nonetheless cold hearted enough to try and hide his part in the boy's death. Pope even keeps quiet when a co-worker Pete (Kevin Hagen) is mistakenly identified as the hit and run driver who killed the paperboy. However, his car has other ideas. It honks its horn, flashes its lights and turns the radio on late at night. It takes on a life of its own and even tries to run Pope down! This spooky car with a conscience is determined to make its owner confess his guilt.

The sequence where the car follows Edward Andrews around a suburban street is well staged and very effective. Haunted car capers are ten a penny in horror cinema but this is a fairly good example of the subgenre. This story was inspired by Hamner Jr's own admitted ineptness with all mechanical devices and suspicion that they held a grudge against him! You Drive is not what you would describe as a Twilight Zone classic but it is fairly absorbing and entertaining and a solid enough season five entry. B

THE LONG MORROW (Director: Robert Florey, Writer: Rod Serling)

"It may be said with a degree of assurance that not everything that meets the eye is as it appears. Case in point: the scene you're watching. This is not a hospital, not a morgue, not a mausoleum, not an undertaker's parlor of the future. What it is is the belly of a spaceship. It is en route to another planetary system an incredible distance from the Earth. This is the crux of our story, a flight into space. It is also the story of the things that might happen to human beings who take a step beyond, unable to anticipate everything that might await them out there. Commander Douglas Stansfield, astronaut, a man about to embark on one of history's longest journeys - forty years out into endless space and hopefully back again. This is the beginning, the first step toward man's longest leap into the unknown. Science has solved the mechanical details, and now it's up to one human being to breathe life into blueprints and computers, to prove once and for all that man can live half a lifetime in the total void of outer space, forty years alone in the unknown. This is Earth. Ahead lies a planetary system. The vast region in between is the Twilight Zone."

An astronaut named Commander Douglas Stansfield (Robert Lansing) is on a forty year space mission he will undertake in suspended animation so that he will not age during his time in space. However, just before he departs he meets and falls in love with Sandra Horn (Mariette Hartley) and while he will return from space having not aged a bit, Sandra will be in her seventies when he gets back...

The Long Morrow starts off great with Lansing in a suspended animation ice cube bath but despite good work by him and Mariette Hartley it soon becomes a trifle bland and far too talky and while the twist is not bad you'll be struggling to retain interest by the time it finally arrives. The Long Morrow always feels like it should be better than it eventually plays. The two nominal leads are good though as the space separated lovers and you may find the bittersweet coda touching.

My main issue with The Long Morrow is that ultimately I find this to be a rather dull and forgettable episode - despite the potentially interesting elements. The main frustration here comes from the fact that expectations are raised by the early and arresting science fiction trappings and Serling's lengthy opening monologue and yet the actual episode thereafter never really grabs your attention or presents you with a story that will linger in the memory afterwards for very long. For this reason The Long Morrow is rather disappointing - all the more so because one can't help feeling this had the potential to be much better. If you are in the mood for a sci-fi love story though you may enjoy this more than I ultimately did in the end. C+

THE SELF-IMPROVEMENT OF SALVADORE ROSS (Director: Don Seigel, Writer: Henry Slesar)

"Confidential personnel file on Salvadore Ross. Personality: a volatile mixture of fury and frustration. Distinguishing physical characteristic: a badly-broken hand which will require emergency treatment at the nearest hospital. Ambition: shows great determination toward self-improvement. Estimate of potential success: a sure bet for a listing in Who's Who in the Twilight Zone."

Salvadore Ross (Don Gordon) is a bad tempered man with no patience. He is furious when his former social worker Leah Maitland (Gail Kobe) rejects his romantic advances and punches a wall in frustration. Now, suffering from a broken hand, he visits the hospital and jokingly remarks to an old man in the bed next to him with a chest cold that he'd love to swap conditions. Later that night, as if by magic, he finds his wish has come true. He has a chest cold while the old man now has his broken hand. He decides to take advantage of this strange new talent...

The Self-Improvement of Salvadore Ross is not a bad episode but it doesn't really make any sense when you think about it afterwards. With the ability to do "swaps" Salvadore exchanges his youth for an old man's fortune and then gets his youth back by getting bellhops to each sell him a year of their life. And so on. Can this bizarre ability win Salvadore happiness and the heart of Leah? The McGuffin here is pretty good and supplies a decent twist but the story never really all comes together and plugs the gaps in logic.

It never feels very realistic for Leah to sway in her feelings for Ross after he was so horrible at the start and the make-up when he is briefly transformed into an elderly man is not terribly convincing. The plot is engagingly gimmicky and ambitious though and The Self-Improvement of Salvadore Ross is at least very watchable. Don Gordon (in his second Twilight Zone appearance) is very good in the lead here too.

This is a solid sort of episode that survives its story shortcomings with a fun central concept and a brisk pace. It's no classic but worth watching all the same.

This is definitely an episode that is difficult to describe given its very 'high concept' sort of premise. B-

NUMBER TWELVE LOOKS JUST LIKE YOU (Director: Abner Biberman, Writer: John Tomerlin (from a story by Charles Beaumont)

"Given the chance, what young girl wouldn't happily exchange a plain face for a lovely one? What girl could refuse the opportunity to be beautiful? For want of a better estimate, let's call it the year 2000. At any rate, imagine a time in the future when science has developed a means of giving everyone the face and body he dreams of. It may not happen tomorrow, but it happens now in the Twilight Zone."

In the future, people undergo a cosmetic procedure at the age of nineteen which makes them beautiful but also (and here's the rub) identical to everyone else. Eighteen year old Marilyn Cuberle (Collin Wilcox) decides that that she wants to avoid the operation and stay the way she is. She is influenced by the memory of her radical father - who believed the operation was a way of enforcing conformity and committed suicide after it was finally done to him...

With a script based on The Beautiful People by Charles Beaumont, Number Twelve Looks Just Like You is an atmospheric glimpse at a terrifying future society where the goal of everyone is to quite literally look the same. Perhaps we might already be starting to live in that society today? This is a great episode made all the more spooky by the fact that because everyone in this future society looks the same several parts are played the same actors. Richard Long is excellent in his various roles, including that of Marilyn's doctor.

The future here is a sterile weird place where people drink Instant Smile when they feel depressed and are encouraged not to think about anything too deeply. Most of all though they are encouraged to all be the same. Literally in this case. Wilcox is excellent in the central part, pleading her case to remain an individual and receiving no sympathy or understanding from anyone. The end is rather chilling and the story is very Stepford Wives too. Marilyn's mother Lana (Suzy Parker) and the staff at the Transformation centre all think Marilyn is mad and worrying herself about nothing. It's all for her own good. Number Twelve Looks Just Like You is a memorable episode about conformity, identity, our concept of beauty, and the pressure to follow the herd when you simply just want to be yourself. A-

BLACK LEATHER JACKETS (Director: Joseph M Newman, Writer: Earl Hamner Jr)

"Three strangers arrive in a small town, three men in black leather jackets in an empty rented house. We'll call them Steve and Scott and Fred, but their names are not important; their mission is, as three men on motorcycles lead us into the Twilight Zone."

Three bikers (played by Le Kinsolving, Michael Forest, and Tom Gilleran) arrive in a small town with leather jackets and sunglasses. They are in fact aliens and part of a first invasion wave with a mission to poison water supplies and kill all humans and animals. They also receive orders from a giant eye that speaks to them through their television set. One of the aliens (who lest we forget are disguised as James Dean type bikers) falls in love with a human named Ellen (Shelley Fabares) when he offers her a lift after she misses the bus. Now, feeling guilty and torn about their mission to wipe out humanity, he has a rethink and is considered a traitor by the other aliens...

One of the weakest episodes in this or any year of The Twilight Zone, Black Leather Jackets never makes a tremendous amount of sense and the stupidity of the aliens (you'd think that if the aliens are trying to be incognito they wouldn't go blustering into town as counter culture bikers and so INEVITABLY attract the attention of the locals!) sinks any leap of faith the viewer might be willing to take. The no name cast aren't given an awful lot of help with the weak script (which is uncharacteristic of the usually reliable Earl Hamner Jr) and the alien invasion portion of the story is so small scale and off-screen they it barely registers.

Black Leather Jackets never really takes off and is full of irritating things that seem stupid. The alien falling in love with a human and then never bothering to prove he is an alien - despite having mystical powers! Ellen thinks he might be a candidate for the funny farm when he claims to be an extraterrestrial and one can't blame her for coming to that conclusion. Black Leather Jackets is pretty hopeless and often cited as one of the worst ever Twilight Zone episode. It's hard to mount much of an argument against that general perception. D

NIGHT CALL (Director: Jacques Tourneur, Writer: Richard Matheson)

"Miss Elva Keene lives alone on the outskirts of London Flats, a tiny rural community in Maine. Up until now, the pattern of Miss Keene's existence has been that of lying in her bed or sitting in her wheelchair reading books, listening to a radio, eating, napping, taking medication, and waiting for something different to happen. Miss Keene doesn't know it yet, but her period of waiting has just ended, for something different is about to happen to her, has in fact already begun to happen, via two most unaccountable telephone calls in the middle of a stormy night, telephone calls routed directly through the Twilight Zone."

An old woman named Elva (Gladys Cooper) begins to receive unsettling telephone calls when she is trying to sleep at night. Where are these spooky calls originating from?

This is a superbly atmospheric and enjoyable ghost story wonderfully directed by Jacques (Cat People) Tourneur. It was an inspired move to get Tourneur involved and he does a great job with the material, slowly amping up the tension and providing nice little flourishes like the shadows of tree branches falling over Elva's face as she lies in bed. Some great detail too during a scene in a cemetery. Night Call is terrific at its best and a stylish little horror yarn.

Gladys Cooper, in her third Twilight Zone appearance, is once again perfectly cast. Night Call is just about the closest The Twilight Zone would ever get in evoking the EC horror comics of the fifties and all the more enjoyable because of it. Horror laced Twilight Zone stories are usually fun and Night Call has a fantastically creepy atmosphere. This is a nice example of how you don't always need an elaborate plot and a huge cast to make a good effective mystery. Night call is definitely one of the most memorable and stylish of the Twilight Zone's excursions into horror and haunted capers. If you like the more scary and spooky episodes of The Twilight Zone you should have fun with this story. B+

FROM AGNES WITH LOVE (Director: Richard Donner, Writer: Bernard C Schoenfeld)

"James Elwood, master programmer, in charge of Mark 502-741, commonly known as 'Agnes', the world's most advanced electronic computer. Machines are made by men for man's benefit and progress, but when man ceases to control the products of his ingenuity and imagination he not only risks losing the benefit, but he takes a long and unpredictable step into the Twilight Zone."

James Elwood (Wally Cox) is a programmer in charge of Mark 502-741 - the most advanced computer in the world and known as "Agnes". Elwood took over the job when the previous programmer was driven insane by Agnes and he soon realises why. The computer gives him romantic suggestions on how to woo fellow office worker Millie (Sue Randall) but none of them go terribly well and Elwood's life is soon in ruin...

A very throwaway episode pitched more as a comedy than anything, From Agnes With Love is not very good and comes across very much as filler in series five. Elwood's attempts to romance office worker Millie never feel especially entertaining and one could argue that the story as a whole isn't exactly dripping in Twilight Zone reside. This is an awful episode really. It tries to be funny but isn't and Wally Cox is far too broad and annoying in the central role.

When Elwood goes on a date with Millie he reads Einstein and complains when she turns the light off so he can hardly complain that the computer's suggestions are wrecking his romantic plans. He seems perfectly capable of doing it himself! There is no twist or any real direction to this episode and it bears the hallmarks of a writer who simply didn't get The Twilight Zone at all. From Agnes - With Love is a weak episode indeed and pretty much a complete waste of time. D+

SPUR OF THE MOMENT (Director: Elliot Silverstein, Writer: Richard Matheson)

"This is the face of terror: Anne Marie Henderson, eighteen years of age, her young existence suddenly marred by a savage and wholly unanticipated pursuit by a strange, nightmarish figure of a woman in black, who has appeared as if from nowhere and now at driving gallop chases the terrified girl across the countryside, as if she means to ride her down and kill her - and then suddenly and inexplicably stops, to watch in malignant silence as her prey takes flight. Miss Henderson has no idea whatever as to the motive for this pursuit; worse, not the vaguest notion regarding the identity of her pursuer. Soon enough, she will be given the solution to this twofold mystery, but in a manner far beyond her present capacity to understand, a manner enigmatically bizarre in terms of time and space, which is to say, an answer from the Twilight Zone."

A young woman named Anne Marie Henderson (Diana Hyland) is terrified and bewildered during her morning country horse ride when an old woman on a stallion pursues her. Anne rushes home where her parents (played by Phillip Ober and Marsha Hunt) are waiting with her sensible stockbroker finance Robert (Robert Hogan). Suddenly, her former fiancee David (Roger Davis) barges in and asks for a second chance and begs Anne not to be forced into marriage by her parents. Her parents disapprove of Robert but will Anne give him a second chance? And who was the woman on the stallion chasing her that morning?

Spur of the Moment is a strange episode that scores marks for atmosphere and weirdness but never really falls into place to become anymore more than a standard season five Twilight Zone. The twist is good but may be spoiled by an early scene if you are eagle eyed and pay attention. Matheson actually complained himself that the big twist in the episode is rather given away at the beginning.

The cast is fine but the episode itself is only average. One suspects Richard Matheson would have expected more to be made of his premise. Spur of the Moment is a nice idea and spooky at times but the episode never really grips as it should. Diana Hyland is certainly good though. Despite the early intrigue of Anne chased by a mad old woman in a cape thundering along on a stallion, Spur of the Moment becomes rather drab and forgettable in the end. There are certainly far worse episodes of The Twilight Zone and completists should give this a try but it might be for the best to lower your expectations going in as this definitely isn't one of the better episodes written by Richard Matheson. C+

AN OCCURRENCE AT OWL CREEK BRIDGE (Director: Robert Enrico, Writer: Ambrose Bierce)

"Tonight a presentation so special and unique that, for the first time in the five years we've been presenting the Twilight Zone, we're offering a film shot in France by others. Winner of the Cannes Film Festival of 1962, as well as other international awards, here is a haunting study of the incredible, from the past master of the incredible, Ambrose Bierce. Here is the French production of An Occurrence at Owl Creek Bridge."

As a Confederate spy (Roger Jacquet) is about to be hung by Union Soldiers over a bridge, he thinks of his beloved wife and how he might possibly escape...

An Occurrence at Owl Creek Bridge (an adaptation of Ambrose Bierce's short story) is a French short film that Cayuga Productions purchased from Europe to show as part of The Twilight Zone because they had to fill an extra slot. It isn't really an official Twilight Zone episode in this sense but a nice bonus film. As the film is practically silent they merely added opening and closing narrations by Rod Serling and it fitted into the Twilight Zone universe remarkably well.

An Occurrence at Owl Creek Bridge is a superb little film with a real earthy and vivid atmosphere and striking music and snare drums by Henri LaNoe. With its haunting twist ending and ethereal atmosphere, An Occurrence at Owl Creek Bridge is a memorable short film and a nice unusual and atypical addition to season five. The film won awards in the short picture category at both the Academy awards and the Cannes Film Festival. The twist at the end is rather devastating and very Twilight Zone in spirit. B+

QUEEN OF THE NILE (Director: John Brahm, Writer: Jerty Sohl and Charles Beaumont)

"Jordan Herrick, syndicated columnist whose work appears in more than a hundred newspapers. By nature a cynic, a disbeliever, caught for the moment by a lovely vision. He knows the vision he's seen is no dream. She is Pamela Morris, renowned movie star, whose name is a household word and whose face is known to millions. What Mr. Herrick does not know is that he has also just looked into the face of the Twilight Zone."

Jordan Herrick (Lee Phillips) is a syndicated columnist for newspapers. His latest assignment is to interview the famous film star Pamela Morris (Ann Blyth) at her mansion. When he arrives he is surprised to find that Pamela looks exactly the same as she did in her famous 1940s movie Queen of the Nile. She doesn't seem to have aged a day. On the way out he is secretly confronted by a woman in her seventies named Viola (Cecila Lousky) - who he takes to be Pamela's mother. But the woman tells him she is actually Pamela's daughter! Jordan decides that it's about time he investigated the mystery of Pamela Morris...

This is the last ever Twilight Zone with a credit for the great Charles Beaumont but he was in poor health by now and most of the work here was really done by Jerry Sohl.

Queen of the Nile is Twilight Zone in second gear but it is fun and the mystery of Pamela (though rather predictable just from the very title of the piece) always retains our interest as Jordan pokes his nose into her affairs trying to work out why she still looks the same today as she did in the 1940s.

Lee Phillips (who previously featured in Passage On the Lady Anne) and Ann Blyth work quite well together in this episode. Queen of the Nile is certainly watchable and the premise is decent enough - although the central theme had already been done much better in Long Live Walter Jameson in the first season of The Twilight Zone. Queen of the Nile is nothing great but pretty decent fun all the same. B-

WHAT'S IN THE BOX (Director: John Brahm, Writer: Martin Goldsmith)

"Portrait of a TV fan. Name: Joe Britt. Occupation: cab driver. Tonight, Mr. Britt is going to watch a really big show, something special for the cabbie who's seen everything. Joe Britt doesn't know it, but his flag is down and his meter's running and he's in high gear on his way to the Twilight Zone."

Joe (William Demarest) Phyllis (Joan Blondell) are boisterous New Yorkers who share an apartment and are usually having an argument. When Joe insults the TV repair man he begins to see alarming visions of the future on the television screen...

What's in the Box is a very throwaway light episode that plays like a sitcom pilot. On the TV screen Joe sees himself with a mistress (which of course he has to shield from his wife) and later sees himself arguing with Phyllis and throwing her out of the window! How can he prevent this alarming future from happening and who was the strange television repairman? The glimpses of the future Joe spies on his television give the episode some impetus and elicit our interest but - on the whole - this is all played much too broadly by the actors. The performances by the two lead actors are very grating and over the top.

What's in the Box might have worked as a straighter and spookier episode but the cast play it like a situation comedy and negate what is a fairly interesting McGuffin. this episode never really comes together and transforms itself into a very good half hour of television although it's not completely unwatchable. One also has a sense here too of two characters being put through the Twilight Zone moral agony booth when they don't really seem to deserve it. What's in the Box is modestly entertaining but largely forgettable in the long run and definitely loses a point or two with the broad approach of the cast. The premise though is sort of fun. C+

THE MASKS (Director: Ida Lupino, Writer: Rod Serling)

"Mr Jason Foster, a tired ancient who on this particular Mardi Gras evening will leave the Earth. But before departing he has some things to do, some services to perform, some debts to pay, and some justice to mete out. This is New Orleans, Mardi Gras time. It is also the Twilight Zone."

Jason Foster (Robert Keith) is about to die and summons his family heirs - Wilfred Harper (Milton Selzer), Emily Harper (Virginia Gregg), Paula Harper (Brooke Hayward), Wilfred Harper Jr (Alan Sues) - over for what will be a strange Mardi Gras ritual. The family are all shallow selfish and loathsome and can't wait for the old man to die so they can get their hands on the money. They don't care about him at all, only the inheritance. Foster says that in order to claim the inheritance they must carry out his final request. They must wear grotesque masks fashioned by a Cajun that reflect their inner selves until midnight. Self-pity, vanity, greed, cruelty, avariciousness. The heirs are aghast at this idea and protest at having to wear the horrible masks but finally agree for the sake of the money. Meanwhile, Foster will wear the mask of death...

The Masks was the only Twilight Zone episode to be directed by a woman - in this case the British born Ida Lupino (who had already been an actress on the show in the first season). Lupino delivers a stylish and wonderfully atmospheric episode but perhaps the real stars of the show are the masks themselves. They are much in the vein of the masks from The Eye of the Beholder and have a strange grotesque beauty.

You can probably see where this story is going to end long before we arrive but it's still a superior episode and one that wouldn't have been out of place in any year of The Twilight Zone. The large cast makes Foster's family appropriately money grabbing and shallow. Robert Keith is excellent as the old man that these vultures all want to die and has some great lines as he lets them know exactly what he thinks of them. "If someone were to cut you open, all they'd find is a cash register." The Masks is a memorable episode and arguably classic Twilight Zone. The only real flaw is that while the twist is very memorable it is rather predictable all the same. B+

I AM THE NIGHT-COLOR ME BLACK (Director: Abner Biberman, Writer: Rod Serling)

"Sheriff Charlie Koch on the morning of an execution. As a matter of fact, it's 7:30 in the morning. Logic and natural laws dictate that at this hour there should be daylight. It is a simple rule of physical science that the sun should rise at a certain moment and supercede the darkness. But at this given moment, Sheriff Charlie Koch, a deputy named Pierce, a condemned man named Jagger and a small, inconsequential village will shortly find out that there are causes and effects that have no precedent. Such is usually the case in the Twilight Zone."

In a small prejudiced town, permanent twenty-four hour darkness mysteriously descends as a man named Jagger (Terry Becker) is about to be wrongfully hung for killing a racist bigot in self-defence. The town was biased towards the idealistic Jagger and his side of the story was not discussed in the local paper. The local sheriff (Michael Constance) knew the case was questionable at best but decided not to do anything about it and leave Jagger to his fate...

Rod Serling wrote this episode in response to the Kennedy assassination and despite the well meaning intentions I Am the Night—Color Me Black emerges as one of the dullest Twilight Zone episodes in the history of the show. Slow, talky, dramatically obvious. The cast are earnest and competent so it's a shame they didn't have a more memorable episode to work with. This is a very pretentious episode that finds Rod Serling on his high horse to no great effect.

The conceit of darkness falling where hate exists feels clunky and the obvious messages of the story are hammered home far too much by the screenplay. All in all I Am the Night—Color Me Black feels like a missed opportunity. It seems very doubtful that this is an episode many would have on their rewatch pile for Twilight Zone marathons. As always, Rod Serling's heart is in the right place but I Am the Night—Color Me Black is simply too dull and heavy-handed. D

SOUNDS AND SILENCES (Director: Richard Donner, Writer: Rod Serling)

"This is Roswell G Flemington, two hundred and twenty pounds of gristle, lung tissue and sound decibels. He is, as you have perceived, a noisy man, one of a breed who substitutes volume for substance, sound for significance, and shouting to cover up the readily apparent phenomenon that he is nothing more than an overweight and ageing perennial Sea Scout whose noise-making is in inverse ratio to his competence and to his character. But soon our would-be admiral of the fleet will embark on another voyage. This one is an unchartered and twisting stream that heads for a distant port called the Twilight Zone."

Roswell G Flemington (John McGiver) is the owner of a model-ship company and obsessed with naval jargon. He's generally a complete loudmouth. His idea of relaxation is playing recordings of naval battles and he is the loudest and most bombastic person you could wish to meet. When his wife (Penny Singleton) leaves him he is ecstatically happy because he can now be as loud as he wants at home. But that night something strange happens and the tiniest noise is suddenly deafening to him...

This is a strange and forgettable episode that finds Serling on very poor form indeed. He was actually accused here of borrowing from a rejected Twilight Zone script that had been submitted two years before. Though this was coincidence more than anything he was clearly almost completely out of fresh ideas by now. There are a few twists in this episode but you'll be past caring by the time they arrive.

John McGiver is fun at first as the blunt and pompous Flemington but his performance quickly becomes ridiculous. There was possibly a decent premise in here somewhere that might have been fashioned into a passable Twilight Zone but Sounds and Silences is as bewildering as any entry in season five. One of the problems with this episode is we don't find the antics of Flemington (who likes to play loud recordings of naval battles and has an incredibly booming voice) very amusing and so both he - and the episode as a whole - merely become irritating. Sounds and Silences is a weak episode indeed. D

CAESAR AND ME (Director: Robert Butler, Writer: Adele T Strassfield)

"Jonathan West, ventriloquist, a master of voice manipulation. A man late of Ireland, with a talent for putting words into other people's mouths. In this case, the other person is a dummy, aptly named Caesar, a small splinter with large ideas, a wooden tyrant with a mind and a voice of his own, who is about to talk Jonathan West into the Twilight Zone."

Jonathan West (Jackie Cooper) is a terrible ventriloquist who is completely broke because his act is so awful. Struggling to pay his rent and with a slender grasp on reality, his creepy dummy Caesar badgers him into committing a series of robberies. But knowledge of his secret robberies soon comes into the possession of his landlady's niece Susan (Morgan Brittany) - a vicious little brat who thinks Jonathan is an idiot and enjoys any power she now has over him...

Ventriloquist under the thrall of his creepy dummy? We've been down this road before many times. Even The Twilight Zone has already done this with the excellent Cliff Robertson episode The Dummy. But, you know what? Caesar and Me is pretty good fun and far more entertaining than the previous few episodes we've had to endure in season five. This is a rather fun episode on the whole and one that always engages one's attention.

Jackie Cooper's Irish accent is risible but his performance is appropriately frazzled and Morgan Brittany is well cast as the smug little girl who decides to make life even more difficult for him. This is notable for being the only Twilight Zone episode written by a woman - in this case the secretary of the producer! They had no scripts lined up so she asked for a bash at writing one and got her wish. Caesar and Me is fun little episode with some decent scenarios of tension. B

THE JEOPARDY ROOM (Director: Richard Donner, Writer: Rod Serling)

"The cast of characters: a cat and a mouse. This is the latter, the intended victim who may or may not know that he is to die, be it by butchery or ballet. His name is Major Ivan Kuchenko. He has, if events go according to certain plans, perhaps three of four more hours of living. But an ignorance shared by both himself and his executioner is of the fact that both of them have taken a first step into the Twilight Zone."

Major Ivan Kuchenko (Martin Landau) is defecting to the West and waits in his hotel room for passage to a safe country. Commissar Vassiloff (John van Dreelenis) is assigned to kill him and intends to do it with the artistry and cunning he is associated with. He intends to make the killing an ingenious work of art. He visits Kuchenko and knocks him out with drugged wine. When Kuchenko comes to a tape recording tells him there is a bomb in the room that he has three hours to find. If he stops looking, turns out the light or tries to leave the room a sniper will shoot him. Can he solve the puzzle?

The Jeopardy Room is a neat, clever and inventive Twilight Zone constructed as a closed room mystery. Kuchenko is given three hours to find a bomb in a hotel room and told that if he tries to leave the room he will shot by a sniper. That's a pretty good scenario for a thriller and the constrictive location makes the story even more tense and claustrophobic. What makes this enjoyable too is that it feels like a slight departure for The Twilight Zone - as if they wanted to try something slightly different.

It's fun to have some Cold War shenanigans in The Twilight Zone here and this story is always compelling and good at holding our attention. The always wonderful Martin Landau is excellent in the main part. This is an absorbing episode with a nice satisfying twist in the tale and great performances by the two lead actors. There is no fantasy at all in The Jeopardy Room but it works really well and always feel very Twilight Zone in terms of its DNA. The Jeopardy Room is a clever and entertaining episode and definitely worthy of your time. B+

STOPOVER IN A QUIET TOWN (Director: Ron Winston, Writer: Earl Hamner Jr)

"Bob and Millie Frazier, average young New Yorkers who attended a party in the country last night and on the way home took a detour. Most of us on waking in the morning know exactly where we are; the rooster or the alarm clock brings up out of sleep into the familiar sights, sounds, aromas of home and the comfort of a routine day ahead. Not so with our young friends. This will be a day like none they've ever spent, and they'll spend it in the Twilight Zone."

New York couple Bob (Barry Nelson) and Millie (Nancy Malone) Frazier groggily wake up in a strange house after a night of heavy drinking. They have no idea where they are or what exactly happened the previous evening - only that they remember a huge shadow appearing over their car at one point but their memories are fogged. They find the house they've woken up in is completely empty. Even stranger is the discovery that the house is filled with fake props like a television studio set. The cupboards are just glued on and the fridge is full of plastic replica food. The bewildered couple wander outside and find themselves in a small town that seems to be completely deserted. Where is everybody? Why does the grass seem to be made of papier-mache? And why do they keep hearing a little girl laughing in the distance?

This is a terrific episode that scores highly for atmosphere and strangeness and even conjures a quite outrageous twist that is silly but pure Twilight Zone. The sense of increasing isolation and entrapment that envelops Bob and Millie (it's especially creepy when they discover a stuffed squirrel in a tree and keep getting on a train that merely takes them back to where they started) is nicely developed and Barry Nelson and Nancy Malone are believable as a bickering married couple who become increasingly spooked by their situation.

The distant laughter of a little girl is also another surreal flourish that adds to the off-kilter ambience. This is one of those Twilight Zones stories that uses isolation and a gradual sense of panic to create a wonderfully atmospheric and strange story. The fact that the couple are quite ordinary and are gently bickering with throbbing hangovers makes them easy to relate to and imagine what it might be like to be their predicament. There are some elements of that David Fincher film The Game here when they find out that the house they are in is full of fake props and the story really becomes gripping when they find that their attempts to leave the town always appear to be doomed.

The sense of atmosphere in Stopover in a Quiet Town comes from the fact that the town is eerily empty and abandoned with only a sense of stillness and quiet apparent. The spooky thing is that the town seems normal on the surface with no sign or panic or flight, it's just empty. This all works well with the somewhat disconcerting sound of the little girl laughing, which the Fraziers keep hearing but can never actually pinpoint despite their best efforts. Isolation was often used to good effect in The Twilight Zone (Where is Everybody?, The Lonely) and Stopover in a Quiet Town is another good example of this recurring theme. B+

THE ENCOUNTER (Director: Robert Butler, Writer: Martin Goldsmith)

"Two men alone in an attic: a young Japanese-American and a seasoned veteran of yesterday's war. It's twenty-odd years since Pearl Harbor, but two ancient opponents are moving into position for a battle in an attic crammed with skeletons: souvenirs, mementos, old uniforms and rusted medals. Ghosts from the dim reaches of the past that will lead us into the Twilight Zone."

World War 2 veteran Fenton (Neville Brand) hires a young man of Japanese heritage named Takamuri (George Takei) to help clean his attic but the discovery of a samurai sword has a most troubling affect on both of them...

The Encounter is a puzzling episode about the ghosts of war and the past, how guilt and vivid memories can remain dormant but powerful when provoked. It devolves into a tiresome piece where the two characters are at each other's throats and overacting abounds. Fenton and Takamuri initially have some beer and Fenton says he'll throw him some cash to help clean the attic. However, Fenton begins to needle Arthur about his Japanese heritage and when they find a samurai sword in the attic it seems to bring out the worst in both of them, triggering flashbacks and old enmities. The pair are soon fighting like Peter Sellers and Burt Kwouk in the Pink Panther films.

You end up feeling like two good actors are wasted in The Encounter in a silly story. Interesting to see a young George Takei here but The Encounter never really engages the viewer or makes an awful lot of sense. The implication that Takei's character was a spy at Pearl Harbour seems rather tasteless too and offensive to Japanese-Americans. The Encounter is a rather baffling and dull episode on the whole and not one you will be in a rush to ever revisit. C

MR GARRITY AND THE GRAVES
(Director: Ted Post, Writer: Rod Serling)

"Introducing Mr Jared Garrity, a gentleman of commerce, who in the latter half of the nineteenth century plied his trade in the wild and woolly hinterlands of the American West. And Mr Garrity, if one can believe him, is a resurrector of the dead - which, on the face of it, certainly sounds like the bull is off the nickel. But to the scoffers amongst you, and you ladies and gentlemen from Missouri, don't laugh this one off entirely, at least until you've seen a sample of Mr Garrity's wares, and an example of his services. The place is Happiness, Arizona, the time about 1890. And you and I have just entered a saloon where the bar whiskey is brewed, bottled and delivered from the Twilight Zone."

In the Old West, an accomplished and polished fraudster named Jared Garrity (John Dehner) arrives in the small town of Happiness and convinces the gullible locals that he can bring back their dead loved ones at the stroke of midnight for $500 each...

This is one of Rod Serling's more successful comic tinged scripts and amusing and nicely played. This episode has a fairly convincing western ambience and John Dehner is great as the title character, delighting in his own scheming and nous as he sets about fleecing the citizens of Happiness. Mr Garrity and the Graves is a lot of fun with Dehner bamboozling the inhabitants of the town with his patter and tricks and then offering them a most extraordinary service. Look out for a wonderfully melodramatic injection of horror late in the episode.

Mr Garrity and the Graves sort of plays like a black and white western episode of Tales from the Crypt with its mix of comedy and horror. This is generally a very watchable and enjoyable episode and among the most memorable of Serling's western themed Twilight Zone scripts. The performance of John Dehner alone is worthy of your time. By the way, I love the detail here that some of the residents of the town don't actually want their deceased relatives back so pay Garrity $500 to keep them dead in the graveyard! The Grave is full of amusing little details like this and a lot of fun. B

THE BRAIN CENTRE AT WHIPPLE'S (Director: Richard Donner, Writer: Rod Serling)

"These are the players, with or without a scorecard: in one corner, a machine; in the other, one Wallace V Whipple, man. And the game? It happens to be the historical battle between flesh and steel, between the brain of man and the product of man's brain. We don't make book on this one, and predict no winner, but we can tell you that for this particular contest there is standing room only in the Twilight Zone."

Wallace V Whipple (Richard Deacon) automates his factory and puts hundreds of men on the unemployment line. His foreman Dickerson (Ted de Corsia) is mortified by this and lets Whipple know that he's a cold hearted crook. Machines can never replace men in his opinion and it's a tragedy that automation and cold hearted bosses are throwing human beings on the scrap heap as if they don't count for anything. Whipple's obsession with machines might be his undoing...

A very weak episode, The Brain Center at Whipple's has an interesting theme at its core but never really goes anywhere and feels half-baked and unfinished. You know you are in trouble when Robby the Robot makes another cameo appearance (his third in The Twilight Zone for those who are counting). The biggest crime this episode commits is to be dull. Whipple's near deserted factory and the lack of much of a supporting cast do not make for the most exciting half hour of television.

The premise of the story here is one that we've already seen in The Twilight Zone - and done better too. Whipple - in the vein of You Drive and A Thing About Machines - will soon discover that mechanical contraptions can be very creepy sometimes and have a life of their own. The Brain Center at Whipple's feels thrown together and aimless and the twist is fairly stupid. The script consists mostly of two men making speeches to one another. The Brain Center at Whipple's is a straight up clunker and pretty hopeless. D

COME WANDER WITH ME (Director: Richard Donner, Writer: Anthony Wilson)

"Mr Floyd Burney, a gentleman songster in search of song, is about to answer the age-old question of whether a man can be in two places at the same time. As far as his folk song is concerned, we can assure Mr Burney he'll find everything he's looking for, although the lyrics may not be all to his liking. But that's sometimes the case when the words and music are recorded in the Twilight Zone."

A famous singer named Floyd Burney (Gary Crosby) travels deep into the country to look for a folk song to use in his act. He meets a strange woman named Mary (Bonnie Beecher) singing an affecting ballad but the song seems to contain warnings about his future...

Come Wander With Me is definitely an eccentric episode (even the director Richard Donner admitted that he couldn't make head nor tail of it) and its whimsical, fantasy, reality, past, present, future blurring and obtuseness (not to mention languid pace) might stretch the patience of viewers but Bonnie Beecher is certainly memorable and the song she sings is genuinely haunting. Gary Crosby is not a tremendously gifted actor on the evidence presented here but he at least believable as a rockabilly star of the era.

This is a genuinely hard episode to describe but one that is at least worth giving a try. Floyd strikes up a friendship and romance with the mystery woman so he can get the song but a man named Billy (John Bolt) arrives looking rather angry and says that he and his brothers know exactly what to do to Floyd. Floyd hits him with a guitar and kills him and - meanwhile - Mary Rachel continues to sing her song but now changing the words so there is a lyric about Floyd's murder of Billy! Oh, and her clothes keep changing too. Even to the point of wearing funeral garb. Come Wander With Me doesn't make any sense whatsoever but it's an experience if nothing else. B-

THE FEAR (Director: Ted Post, Writer: Rod Serling)

"The major ingredient of any recipe for fear is the unknown. And here are two characters about to partake of the meal: Miss

Charlotte Scott, a fashion editor, and Mr. Robert Franklin, a state trooper. And the third member of the party: the unknown, that has just landed a few hundred yards away. This person or thing is soon to be met. This is a mountain cabin, but it is also a clearing in the shadows known as the Twilight Zone."

Trooper Franklin (Peter Mark Richman) is called out to visit the remote cabin of Miss Scott (Hazel Court) - a scared woman who is recovering from a nervous breakdown and has reported strange lights in the sky. Turns out that something weird is indeed going on. Franklin's car is rolled over, there is blinding light outside, the telephone line goes down, the radio doesn't work. Could the gigantic footprints they find outside have anything to do with it?

The Fear doesn't seem to have much of a reputation as far as Twilight Zone episodes go but I have something of a soft spot for it. The Fear has a truly preposterous climax but if you can get past that it's a very solid late addition to the series with the mystery activity around Miss Scott's cabin (which include huge footprints) maintaining our curiosity and a good sense of atmosphere conveyed by the director.

The verbal exchanges between the two leads are a bit too purple at times but it does give the actors something to do and provides a few sparks. Would a country State Trooper really be as talkative and articulate as Peter Mark Richman is here? I'd imagine he'd want to get to the root of the problem and report back rather than banter bons mots in a cabin somewhere. Anyway, the episode becomes quite enjoyable and gripping when the strange events occur and Franklin ventures out to see what is going on. The Fear is pretty entertaining as far as it goes. This is far from a classic Twilight Zone episode but it's sort of fun, evoking The Monsters Are Due On Maple Street and The Invaders - even if it falls far below the standard set by those two earlier stories. B

THE BEWITCHIN' POOL (Director: Joseph M Newman, Writer: Earl Hamner Jr)

"A swimming pool not unlike any other pool, a structure built of tile and cement and money, a backyard toy for the affluent, wet entertainment for the well-to-do. But to Jeb and Sport Sharewood, this pool holds mysteries not dreamed of by the building contractor, not guaranteed in any sales brochure. For this pool has a secret exit that leads to a never-neverland, a place designed for junior citizens who need a long voyage away from reality, into the bottomless regions of the Twilight Zone."

Sport (Mary Badham) and Jeb (Tim Stafford) are two children fed up with their bickering parents. They like to hang out in the back garden where is a huge swimming pool. One afternoon a boy with an anachronistic Huckelberry Finn appearance appears in the pool and beckons them to follow. They dive in after him and surface in some backswoods creek where there are a number of children playing happily with no adults to annoy them. They seem to have been transported to some child's paradise presided over by a warm loving Earth Mother granny named Aunt T (Georgia Simmons). Will the children want to go back to their parents or stay here?

The last ever episode of the original and classic Twilight Zone. This feels more like a pilot for a children's television show than a Twilight Zone story and suffers from a number of problems. Mary Badham (of To Kill A Mockingbird) is dubbed, the children have silly names and different accents from their parents!, and Rod Serling does not two but THREE narrations to plug the fact they didn't have enough material to spin the episode out. What happens to the children in this mystical backswoods paradise? Do they grow up or remain children forever like Peter Pan? I've no idea.

The magical child's paradise the children escape to is a bit hokey it has to be said but Georgia Simmons is well cast as the warmhearted Aunt T (who seems to be a surrogate mother to these children). It's probably best not to ask too many questions of The Bewitchin' Pool because it won't answer any of them. The Bewitchin' Pool is mildly watchable but not a memorable episode. It feels rather unfinished and rushed and is probably not something you will feel compelled to return to once you've seen it. This is a rather disappointing end to what is a patchy final season for The Twilight Zone. Season five will often stretch your patience but - thankfully - the rewards offered by the likes of Nightmare at 20,000 Feet, In Praise of Pip, Number Twelve Looks Just Like You, The Masks, Night Call, and Stopover in a Quiet Town do make it worth exploring. C+

FINAL LISTS

Here, in no particular order, is my own personal list of the ten
best episodes of The Twilight Zone...

TO SERVE MAN
WALKING DISTANCE
A STOP AT WILLOUGHBY
THE AFTER HOURS
THE MIDNIGHT SUN
IT'S A GOOD LIFE
WILL THE REAL MARTIAN PLEASE STAND UP?
MINIATURE
ON THURSDAY WE LEAVE FOR HOME
NIGHTMARE AT 20,000 FEET

In no particular order, here are (in my humble opinion) the
other Twilight Zone classics most worthy of your time...

NICK OF TIME
THE INVADERS
THE LONELY
TIME ENOUGH AT LAST
THIRD FROM THE SUN
DEATHS-HEAD REVISITED
LONG LIVE WALTER JAMESON
THE HOWLING MAN
KICK THE CAN
A HUNDRED YARDS OVER THE RIM
A GAME OF POOL
THE ODYSSEY OF FLIGHT 33
FIVE CHARACTERS IN SEARCH OF AN EXIT
NUMBER TWELVE LOOKS JUST LIKE YOU

The best of the rest - in no particular order, these are my
personal favourites out of the remaining episodes...

THE RIP VAN WINKLE CAPER
LITTLE GIRL LOST
WHERE IS EVERYBODY?
AND WHEN THE SKY WAS OPENED
THE LITTLE PEOPLE
DEATH SHIP
THE HITCH-HIKER
MIRROR IMAGE
STOPOVER IN A QUIET TOWN
THE SILENCE
THE MONSTERS ARE DUE ON MAPLE STREET
IN PRAISE OF PIP
PEOPLE ARE ALIKE ALL OVER
NIGHT CALL
THE NEW EXHIBIT
THE DUMMY
A PASSAGE FOR TRUMPET
THE MASKS
PRINTER'S DEVIL
THE TROUBLE WITH TEMPLETON
THE EYE OF THE BEHOLDER
SHADOW PLAY
THE CHANGING OF THE GUARD
IN HIS IMAGE

The bottom of the barrel! Here, in no particular order, are my least favourite Twilight Zone episodes...

MR BEVIS
SHOWDOWN WITH RANCE McGREW
THE MIRROR
BLACK LEATHER JACKETS
THE LAST NIGHT OF A JOCKEY
THE GIFT
FOUR O'CLOCK
I AM THE NIGHT-COLOR ME BLACK
CAVANDER IS COMING

HE'S ALIVE
SOUNDS AND SILENCES
UNCLE SIMON
FROM AGNES WITH LOVE
MR DINGLE, THE STRONG
THE WHOLE TRUTH
THE BRAIN CENTRE AT WHIPPLE'S

REFERENCES

The opening narrations were taken from twilightzone.fandom.com/wiki.